AGS
GEOGRAPHY
of the United States

by
Milbrey Zelley, M.A.

AGS®

American Guidance Service, Inc.
4201 Woodland Road
Circle Pines, MN 55014-1796
1-800-328-2560

X 30080

Learning About Our United States

Cover photo credit: Images © 1996 Photo Disc, Inc.

Printed in the United States of America

ISBN 0–7854–0959–9 (Previously ISBN 0–88671–971–2)

Order Number: 90870

A 0 9 8

Contents

Unit 5:   Regions

What Is Geography?

Geography is the study of the earth and its resources and the way in which people use those resources. Geographers—people who use geography to find out things—deal with people's adaptation to a variety of conditions, both natural and people-developed. They are interested in the places where things happen and why those things happen in the particular places where they do. For example, geographers might want to know why people chose a certain area for building a city. They want to know what characteristics of that place make it ideal for a city. Does it have access to a good water supply? Is it near a harbor or a river? Does it have access to good farmland and plenty of food for the city's citizens?

◼ Read the questions below and write the answers.

1. What is *geography?* _____

_____

2. What are two things that interest geographers?

   a. _____

   _____

   b. _____

   _____

3. What two reasons might make people choose a particular place to build a city?

   a. _____

   _____

   b. _____

   _____

4. What is there about the place where you live that might make people decide to live there?

_____

_____

Before geographers can begin to look for answers to the question of why things happen where they do, they have to know where things happen. To find places where things happen, geographers depend upon maps. A *map* is a representation of a real place on the earth's surface. It gives information about bodies of water, landforms, and objects made by people, such as roads and railroads. It tells where the place being mapped is located on the surface of the earth. A map is the geographer's most important tool. To become skilled at geography, you must learn how to read and use maps.

You need to know how to tell directions on a map. Most maps have a drawing called a *compass.* This compass tells you which direction is north. Another name for the compass is the *compass rose.*

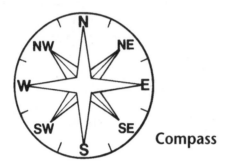

Compass

Notice that in addition to telling you which direction is north, the compass also tells you the other three *cardinal,* or main, directions: south, east, and west. Sometimes intermediate points are also given: northeast, southeast, southwest, and northwest.

A See if you can figure out which direction is south, east and west on the map below. First find and circle the compass. Write the words *south, east,* and *west* next to the appropriate letters on the edges of the map.

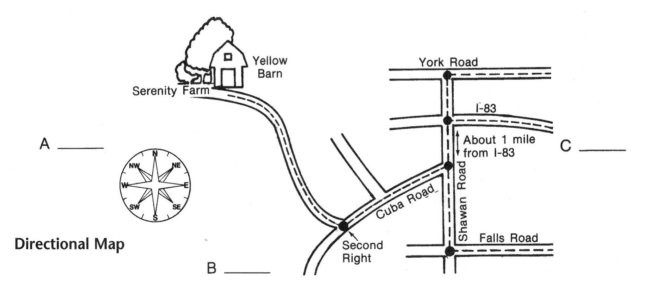

Directional Map

B Find and circle the compass. Write the words *south, east,* and *west* near the appropriate letters on the edges of the map.

Treasure Map

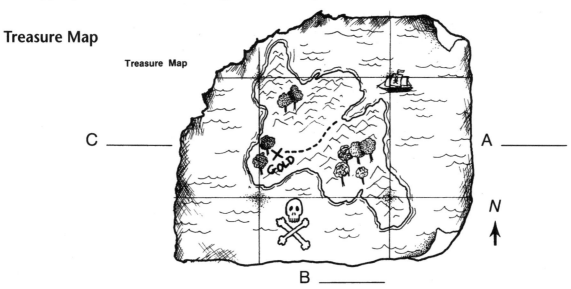

C You have just found gold at the spot marked **X** on the map above. Circle the correct letter and answer the question.

1. If you stand facing north, where is south?
   a. In front of you
   b. In back of you
   c. On your left side

2. What is south of you?

   _____

3. If you stand facing east, where is north?
   a. In front of you
   b. On your left side
   c. On your right side

4. What is north of you?

   _____

5. If you stand facing south, where is west?
   a. In front of you
   b. On your left side
   c. On your right side

6. What is west of you?

   _____

7. If you stand facing west, where is east?
   a. In front of you
   b. In back of you
   c. On your right side

8. What is east of you?

   _____

9. If you stand facing north, where is east?
   a. To your right
   b. To your left
   c. In back of you

10. What direction do you go to return to

    your ship? _____

Map Grids

Geographers have designed a method of locating places that is based on a simple idea: a grid system. A *grid* is just a set of numbered and/or lettered squares. Each square is given two numbers or one number and one letter. One tells how far above or below the starting point the square is. The other tells how far to the right or the left of the starting point the square is.

A To see how this simple system works, try the practice exercise below. Mark the place for each building on this grid. The first one is done for you.

1. The Fox Building is located in D2.

2. The Medical Building is located in H3.

3. The Treasury Building is located in B1 and B2.

4. The court building is located in G1 and H1.

5. The police station is located in A1.

	A	B	C	D	E	F	G	H	I	J	K
1											
2				**X**							
3											

B Lines on a street map can work the same way. Mark the locations described below. The first one is done for you.

1. First Street crosses Main Street in C3.

2. First Street crosses Elm Street near E1 and F1.

3. Oak Street dead ends in G6.

4. Farm Way leaves town near K1.

5. Main Street crosses Elm Street in G4.

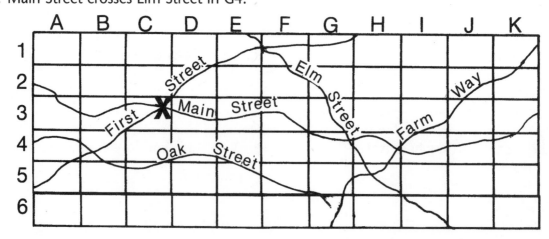

Latitude and Longitude

Geographers have their own special grid system to find places on the earth. They have drawn imaginary lines on the earth's surface. The lines that go across the earth's surface are called *lines of latitude.* They are measured from the zero degree line of latitude, which is called the *equator.* There are 90 degrees (90°) of latitude between the equator and the north pole and 90 degrees (90°) of latitude between the equator and the south pole.

A Put an X on the map to mark the following lines.

1. the equator

2. 60° north of the equator

3. 20° south of the equator

Latitude

The lines that go up and down on the earth's surface are called *lines of longitude.* They are measured from the zero degree meridian, called the *prime meridian.* There are 180 degrees of longitude east of the prime meridian and 180 degrees of longitude west of the prime meridian.

B Put an X on the map to mark the following lines. Then complete the sentence.

1. the prime meridian

2. 100° west of the prime meridian

3. 60° east of the prime meridian

4. The United States is

_____ of the

equator and

_____ of the

prime meridian.

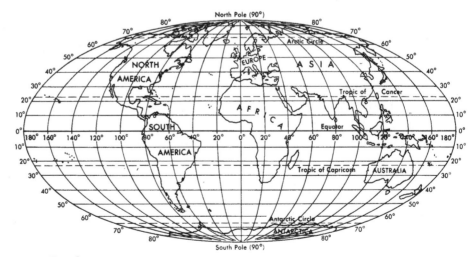

Longitude

Using the Grid System

We are now going to practice using the geographer's grid system of lines of longitude and latitude to locate places in the United States.

Remember that latitude measures how far north and south of the equator a place is, and longitude measures how far east or west of the prime meridian a place is.

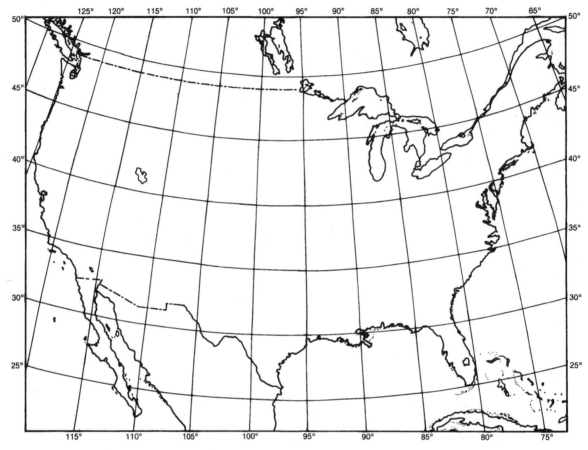

Grid System Using Longitude and Latitude

Above is a map of the 48 contiguous states (states whose borders touch other states). Use this map to answer the questions below.

1. At what longitude line is the most eastern point of the 48 states? _____

2. At what longitude line is the most western point of the 48 states? _____

3. At what latitude line is the most northern point of the 48 states? _____

4. At what latitude line is the most southern point of the 48 states? _____

5. For how many degrees do the 48 states reach from east to west? _____

6. For how many degrees do the 48 states reach from north to south? _____

Locating United States Cities

This lesson will give you further practice using the geographer's grid system of latitude and longitude lines. Below is a map of the 48 contiguous states.

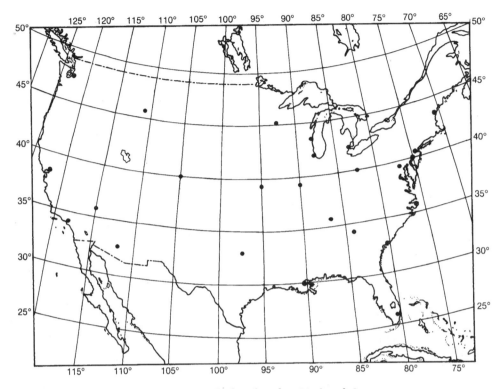

Cities in the United States

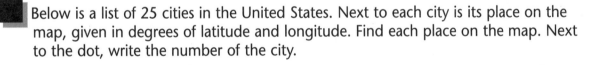

Below is a list of 25 cities in the United States. Next to each city is its place on the map, given in degrees of latitude and longitude. Find each place on the map. Next to the dot, write the number of the city.

1. Atlanta, Georgia 34°N 84°W
2. Boston, Massachusetts 43°N 71°W
3. Columbus, Ohio 40°N 83°W
4. Denver, Colorado 40°N 105°W
5. Detroit, Michigan 42°N 83°W
6. Chicago, Illinois 42°N 88°W
7. Los Angeles, California 34°N 118°W
8. Seattle, Washington 48°N 122°W
9. Dallas, Texas 33°N 97°W
10. New Orleans, Louisiana 30°N 90°W
11. Miami, Florida 26°N 81°W
12. New York, New York 41°N 74°W
13. St. Louis, Missouri 39°N 90°W

14. Kansas City, Kansas 39°N 95°W
15. Washington, D.C. 39°N 77°W
16. Minneapolis, Minnesota 45°N 93°W
17. Las Vegas, Nevada 36°N 115°W
18. Charleston, South Carolina 33°N 80°W
19. Philadelphia, Pennsylvania 40°N 75°W
20. San Francisco, California 38°N 122°W
21. Milwaukee, Wisconsin 43°N 88°W
22. Nashville, Tennessee 36°N 87°W
23. Phoenix, Arizona 33°N 112°W
24. Norfolk, Virginia 36°N 76°W
25. Helena, Montana 47°N 112°W

Another type of map that is familiar to most of us is a *weather map.* Weather maps are often printed in daily newspapers. They show what the weather conditions for the day are all over the United States. The weather map tells what the high temperature in a place is likely to be. It also tells whether or not there is likely to be any precipitation (rain, snow, sleet, or hail). Below is a typical weather map of the United States.

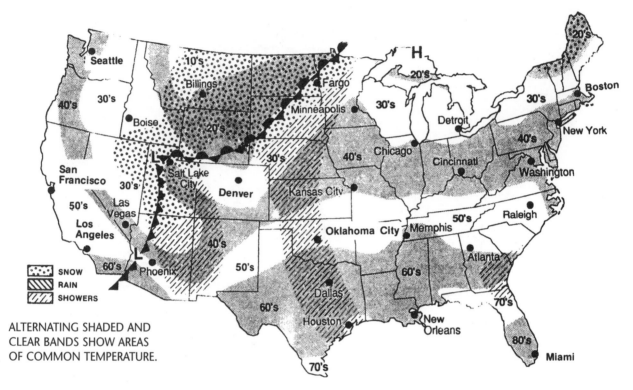

ALTERNATING SHADED AND
CLEAR BANDS SHOW AREAS
OF COMMON TEMPERATURE.

High Temperatures and Precipitation

Answer the questions below.

1. What kinds of precipitation are shown in the map key?

   a. _____

   b. _____

   c. _____

2. What do the numbers of the map tell? _____

   _____

3. What is the coldest temperature shown on this map? _____

4. What is the warmest temperature shown on this map? _____

5. Which city shown on this map has the warmest temperature?_____

6. What four cities on the map will have temperatures in the 30's?

   a. _____

   b. _____

   c. _____

   d. _____

7. What cities will probably have snow?

   _____

   _____

8. What cities may have showers?

   _____

   _____

9. What will the temperature be in:

   a. San Francisco? _____

   b. Denver?_____

   c. Dallas?_____

   d. Chicago?_____

   e. Raleigh? _____

   f. New Orleans? _____

   g. New York? _____

   h. Boston?_____

   i. your city or town? _____

10. When might the information on a weather map be useful to you?

   _____

   _____

   _____

   _____

   _____

   _____

Physical Maps

Geographers use maps to show many different things about the earth and the way people live on the earth. They use maps to show what the surface of the earth looks like. They use what are called *physical maps* to show oceans, lakes, and rivers. These maps also show mountains, valleys, and plains or flat lands.

 Study the physical map below and identify the surface features.

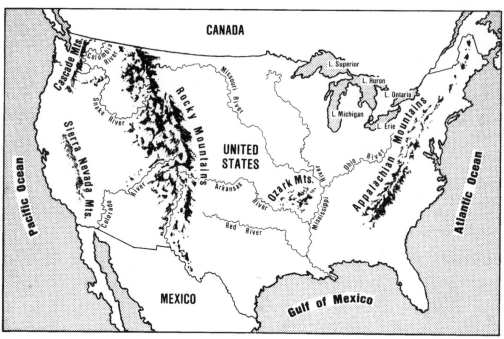

Physical Map of the United States

1. Name five of the rivers shown on this map.

   a. _____   c. _____   e. _____

   b. _____   d. _____

2. Name the two oceans shown on this map.

   a. _____   b. _____

3. Name the five lakes shown on this map.

   a. _____   c. _____   e. _____

   b. _____   d. _____

4. Name the four largest mountain ranges shown on this map.

   a. _____   c. _____

   b. _____   d. _____

Special Maps

A map can be used to show many different kinds of data. The most familiar maps show political information, like the boundaries of states, the locations of cities, and major routes of transportation. However, geographers make use of maps to help them understand the locations of natural resources. They also use maps to help them understand the locations of various kinds of farming. Sometimes maps show where people of different nationalities live. Sometimes they show where people with different incomes live. Studying the information on different kinds of maps gives us a better understanding of what is happening in our country. It helps us understand why things happen where they do.

A Study the map. Then answer the questions below.

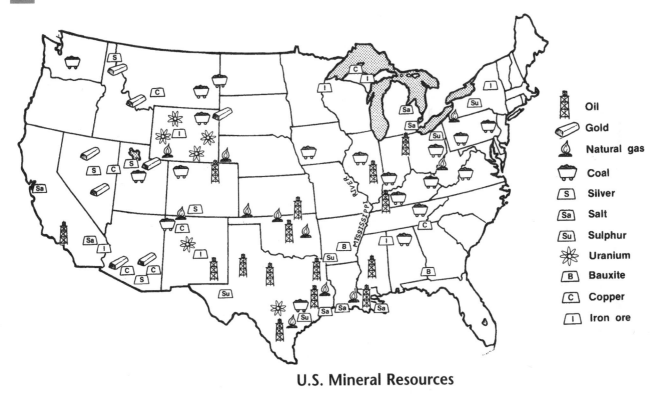

U.S. Mineral Resources

1. What is the title of the map? _____

2. What does the map show?_____

3. Is there more coal east or west of the Mississippi River?_____

4. What is the symbol for iron? _____ What is the symbol for gold? _____

5. How many states have silver deposits? _____

6. Why are resources important to a region? to our country? _____

_____

B Study the map. Then answer the questions below.

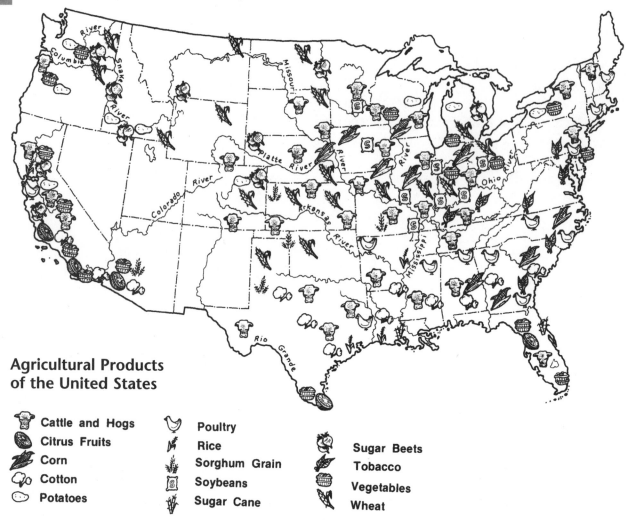

**Agricultural Products
of the United States**

🐄 Cattle and Hogs   🐔 Poultry

🍋 Citrus Fruits   Rice   Sugar Beets

🌽 Corn   Sorghum Grain   Tobacco

Cotton   Ⓢ Soybeans   Vegetables

Potatoes   Sugar Cane   Wheat

1. What is the title of this map?

_____

2. List six crops shown on this map.

_____

3. Mark with an X the states that have fewer than two agricultural products.

4. Why do you think these states have so few agricultural products?

_____

_____

5. Circle the state in the western United States that has the greatest variety of agricultural products.

6. Why do you think this state has such a great variety of products?

_____

7. What is the map symbol for:

a. potatoes? _____   d. poultry? _____

b. cattle and hogs? _____   e. sugar beets? _____

c. cotton? _____   f. tobacco? _____

8. How many symbols for soybeans are on the map? _____

9. You are driving along the eastern coast from Maine to Florida.
   What different kinds of agricultural products would you see?

a. _____   e. _____

b. _____   f. _____

c. _____   g. _____

d. _____   h. _____

10. In what part of the United States is most of the cotton grown?

_____

11. Look at the states that produce cotton. Do you think cotton requires a long
    or a short growing season? Why?

_____

_____

12. Do farmers in the United States raise more poultry or more cattle and hogs?

_____

13. Are more vegetables grown east or west of the Mississippi?

_____

14. Why are agricultural products important to our country?

_____

_____

_____

_____

When President Thomas Jefferson purchased the Louisiana Territory from France in 1803, this large area was added to the United States. The President sent two explorers, Meriwether Lewis and William Clark, to cross the North American continent. He wanted these two men to explore this new area of the United States and find out what it was like.

Lewis and Clark began their journey across the continent in 1804. They followed the Missouri River northwest from St. Louis on the Mississippi River. As they traveled, they made maps of the region. They made drawings of the Indians they met and the plants and animals they saw. They kept a careful record of their entire trip.

Lewis and Clark crossed the Rocky Mountains in what are now the states of Montana and Idaho. From there, they followed the Columbia River to the Pacific Ocean. After wintering on the coast, they traveled back to St. Louis. These explorers opened the way to the Pacific Northwest region. Many thousands of Americans in the next 50 years made their homes west of the Rocky Mountains in the Pacific Northwest.

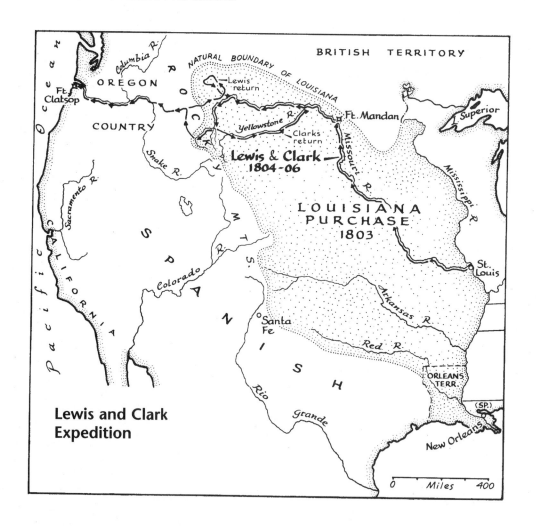

Lewis and Clark Expedition

A Study the map on page 18 and answer the questions below.

1. What city did the Lewis and Clark expedition leave from?

_____

_____

2. What three major river systems did these explorers follow?

_____

_____

_____

3. What mountain range did these explorers cross?

_____

_____

4. Why do you think that Lewis and Clark made maps of their route to the Pacific coast?

_____

_____

_____

5. How do you think the maps Lewis and Clark made helped later settlers in the Pacific Northwest?

_____

_____

_____

Map Made by Lewis and Clark

B If the statement below is true, write *T* in the blank. If it is false, write *F*.

_____ 1. One year after President Jefferson bought the Louisiana Territory, Lewis and Clark were sent to explore it.

_____ 2. They explored the continent of South America.

_____ 3. They took photos of Indians.

_____ 4. Lewis and Clark drew careful, detailed maps and kept accurate records.

_____ 5. They did not make it across the Rocky Mountains.

_____ 6. They reached the Hudson River.

_____ 7. Lewis and Clark contributed valuable information that would help Americans settle in the West.

Locating Roads

All over the United States, Americans have built roads. Have you ever wondered why they built these roads where they did? What makes one place a better location for a road than another place? Roads, of course, connect one location with another. Usually highway planners consider cost and safety. They try to put the road on land that will not be too difficult to build on. They look for a route that will not have to have too many bridges or that does not have too many steep hills. Yet they also want the route to be the shortest distance possible. When highway planners survey an area for a road, they try to combine these two qualities. They look for a route that will be a combination of the shortest possible distance with the least building or engineering difficulties.

The map in this lesson shows a part of Yellowstone National Park. The map shows surface features of the park such as rivers, mountains, and lakes. It also shows the main roads through the park. As you study the map, see if you can figure out why the roads were built where they were.

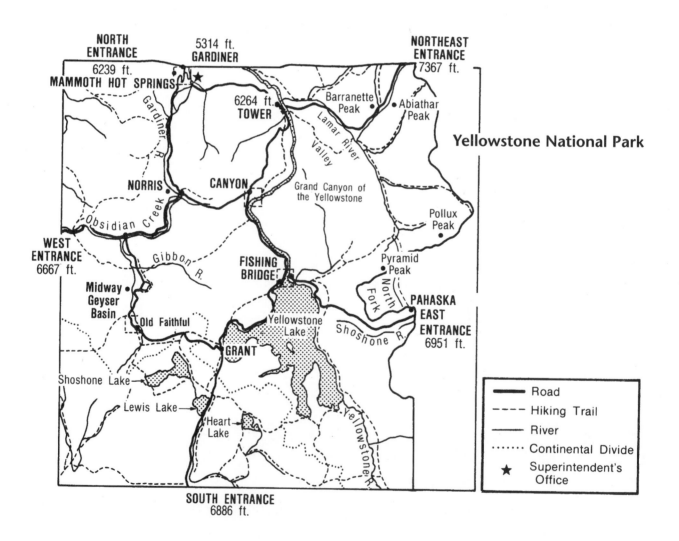

Study the map of Yellowstone Park. Then answer the questions.

1. What surface feature runs parallel to the road at the North Entrance?

_____

2. Just beyond the superintendent's office at Mammoth Hot Springs, the road makes a sharp curve. What do you think the land is like at this location? (Hint: Notice the elevation or height of Gardiner and Mammoth.)

_____

3. Between Mammoth Hot Springs and Canyon, how many bridges had to be built across the Gardiner River and Obsidian Creek?

_____

4. If you entered the park at the Northeast Entrance, what surface features would you see for most of the drive to Tower?

_____

5. If you entered the park at the East Entrance, what surface features would your road follow?

_____

6. If you hiked along the trail (see dotted line) that starts north from Pahaska, where do you think the hike would be most difficult?

_____

What makes this place a difficult area to hike in?

_____

7. This trail runs above a river canyon. If the Park Service decided to replace this trail with a road for automobiles, why would building this road be difficult?

_____

8. What surface feature parallels the road from Grant Village to Fishing Bridge?

_____

9. Most of the roads in the park follow rivers and creeks. Why do you think the roads were built there?

_____

10. Why can't you drive along the Grand Canyon of the Yellowstone?

_____

Cities and Towns

There are many different reasons why towns and cities are located where they are. Sometimes a town was started in a certain place because there was a good harbor nearby. Sometimes a town began to grow because there was a waterfall nearby providing power for a mill. Sometimes a town grew into a city because a lot of roads met there, making it easy for buyers and sellers to get together to do business.

Most towns and cities have grown gradually. However, sometimes people decide to plan an entire town from scratch. These planned communities, as they are called, include industrial areas, shopping centers, and many different kinds of housing.

Columbia, Maryland, is an example of such a planned community. In 1963, the Rouse Company bought 14,000 acres of farmland in Howard County, Maryland. The company told the people of Howard County that it was going to build a new city. It said that this city would provide jobs and recreation for the people who moved there. There would be schools, shopping centers, and hospitals for the people.

By 1990s, there were over 75,000 people living in Columbia. They find that the city is in a good location. What makes Columbia's location so ideal?

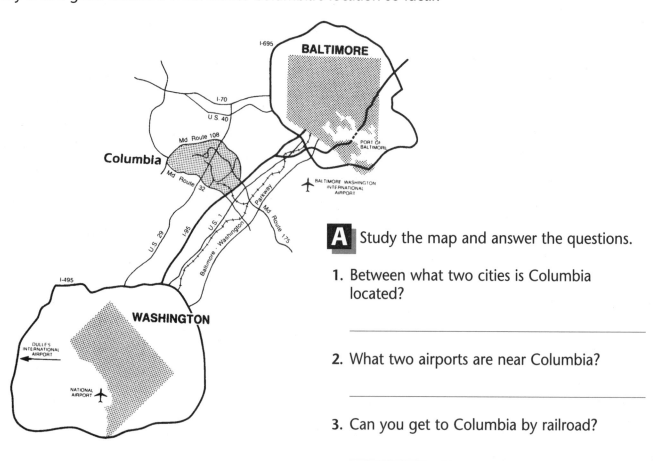

A Study the map and answer the questions.

1. Between what two cities is Columbia located?

   _____

2. What two airports are near Columbia?

   _____

3. Can you get to Columbia by railroad?

   _____

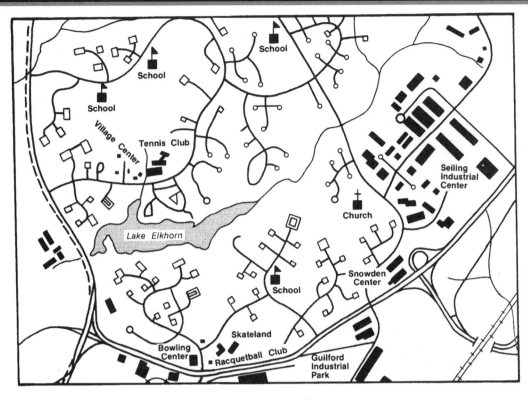

**Village
of Owen Brown,
Columbia**

B Study this map and the one on page 22 and answer the questions.

1. What direction would you go to get to Washington, D.C., from Columbia? _____

2. What U.S. highway goes through the middle of Columbia? _____

3. What interstate highway borders Columbus? _____

4. Where could you go shopping in the village of Owen Brown? _____

5. Why do you think Guilford Industrial Park and Seiling Industrial Center are
   located on the outskirts of the community?

   _____

6. How many schools are there in Owen Brown? _____

7. What recreational facilities are located in Owen Brown?

   _____

8. Why do you think the planners built a lake in the village?

   _____

   _____

9. Does Columbia have room to grow? Why or why not?

   _____

Shopping Centers

How many of you have ever shopped in a shopping mall? A *shopping mall* is a group of stores located in one place. The mall has parking spaces for its customers. Some shopping malls have only a few stores. Sometimes, though, a shopping mall has more than a hundred different stores.

These stores are connected to each other by an area for shoppers to walk in. This area usually has a roof so that shoppers can go from one store to another without having to go outside. Sometimes there are benches, fountains, pools, and even trees planted in the mall, which makes it look like an inside park.

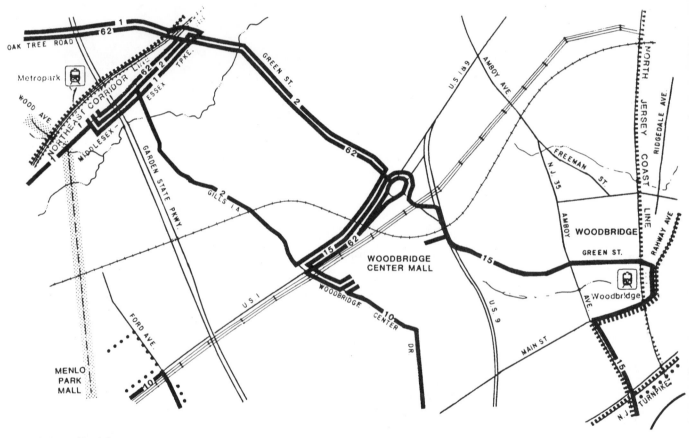

Woodbridge

Woodbridge Mall in Woodbridge, New Jersey, is an inside mall with many stores for shoppers to choose from. It has restaurants and big department stores. It also has many specialty shops like shoe stores, toy shops, drugstores, and clothing stores. In fact, you can buy almost anything at Woodbridge Mall.

Around the mall is a huge parking lot that can hold thousands of cars. The builders of Woodbridge Mall knew that many people would drive their cars to the mall. They knew this because of where the mall is located. Look at the map on page 24. See if you can figure out why so many people drive their cars to Woodbridge Mall.

■ Study the map on page 24 and then answer the questions.

1. If you were driving south on the Garden State Parkway, where would you get off to reach Woodbridge Mall?

_____

_____

2. If you were driving on the New Jersey Turnpike, how would you get to Woodbridge Mall?

_____

_____

3. What two U.S. highways are next to Woodbridge Mall?

a. _____   b. _____

The map shows where Woodbridge Mall is located in New Jersey. Several million people live within 30 miles of Woodbridge Mall.

4. Why do you think Woodbridge Mall was built where it is?

_____

_____

_____

5. If there is a mall near where you live, what streets or highways do you use to get there?

_____

_____

_____

UNIT 1

In 1973, what was then the world's largest jumbo jet airport opened for business. The airport is the Dallas/Fort Worth Airport. It covers 17,500 acres, an area larger than Manhattan Island in New York City!

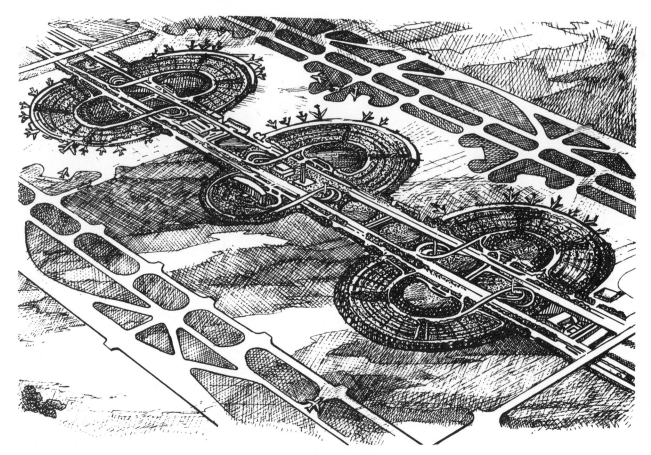

Dallas/Fort Worth Airport

When the plans for an airport were first made, builders looked for a special kind of place to put it. They wanted a place that could be reached easily by many people. They wanted a place where land was available and not too expensive.

The land finally chosen for the airport was once farmland in Grapevine, Texas. This land was chosen for the airport because of its location. It is between two large and important cities, Dallas and Fort Worth. These cities are 34 miles apart. Builders of the airport chose Grapevine so that people from both cities would be able to get to the airport easily. They also chose Grapevine because at the time, the land there was plentiful and cheap. With so much land surrounding the airstrips, people who lived in the nearby area would not be bothered by noise from the airplanes as they landed and took off. Grapevine, Texas, was a suitable site for the new airport.

Use the information on page 26 to answer these questions.

1. What three things did the builders look for when they were choosing a site for the airport?

   a. _____

   b. _____

   c. _____

2. What two cities are near the airport?

   a. _____   b. _____

3. Why do you think the builders wanted to build the airport near these two cities?

   _____

   _____

4. Why do you think the builders needed to be able to buy the land for the airport cheaply?

   _____

   _____

5. Why did the builders want such a large amount of land for the airport?

   _____

   _____

   _____

6. What made Grapevine, Texas, a good site for the new airport?

   _____

   _____

   _____

In Unit 2, you will study two topics. The first is what geographers call the physical characteristics of the United States. The term *physical characteristics* means what the land is like, what the climate is like, and what plants grow on the land. The second topic you will learn about is the human characteristics of the citizens of the United States. *Human characteristics* means what the people who live in the United States are like.

This lesson is about the main landforms or kinds of landforms in the United States. The highest landforms in the United States are its mountains. There are five major mountain *ranges* in the United States. One of these is the Appalachian Mountains. This range is long, stretching from Alabama and Georgia north to Maine. Even though the whole range is called the Appalachians, these mountains have different names in different states. For example, in Tennessee and North Carolina they are called the Great Smoky Mountains. In Vermont they are called the Green Mountains. The other four main mountain ranges are west of the Mississippi River. They are the Ozark Mountains in Arkansas and Missouri; the Rocky Mountains, which go from New Mexico north to Montana; the Sierra Nevada Mountains on the California-Nevada border, and the Cascade Range in Washington and Oregon.

A Match the mountain ranges in Column A with their locations in Column B by writing the correct letter in the blank.

Column A	Column B
_____ 1. Rocky Mountains	**a.** Oregon and Washington
_____ 2. Ozark Mountains	**b.** Missouri and Arkansas
_____ 3. Cascade Range	**c.** Alabama to Maine
_____ 4. Appalachian Mountains	**d.** New Mexico to Montana
_____ 5. Sierra Nevada Mountains	**e.** Nevada and California

Mountains are not the only landforms in the United States. There are level stretches of land called *plains*. Many parts of the United States are plains. Plains are found along the Atlantic Coast and the coast of the Gulf of Mexico. Plains called the *Central Lowlands* are found around the Great Lakes. The area west of the Mississippi River and east of the Rocky Mountains is known as the *Great Plains*. The area between the Rocky Mountains and the Sierra Nevada Mountains is called the *Great Basin*.

B Study the landform map of the United States. On the map, label each of the following landforms by number.

1. The Atlantic Coastal Plains
2. The Great Plains
3. The Appalachian Mountains
4. The Central Lowlands
5. The Rocky Mountains

6. The Great Basin
7. The Sierra Nevadas
8. The Cascade Range
9. The Ozark Mountains
10. The Gulf Coastal Plain

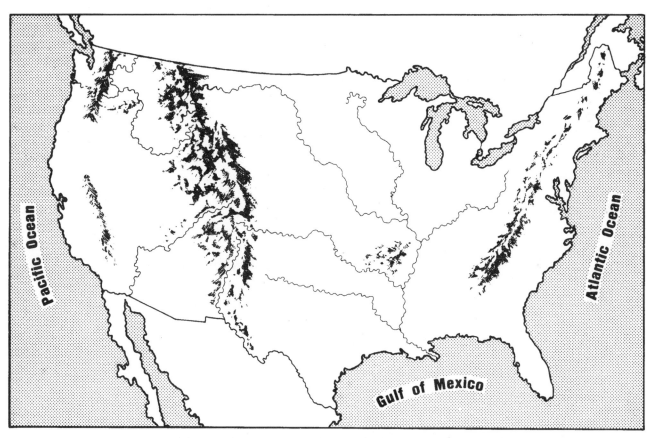

Landform Map of the United States

Water Systems in the United States

The United States is a country of many rivers and lakes. In this lesson, you will learn the names and locations of some of the largest of these water systems. You will also learn some ways in which these water systems are important to the people who live near them.

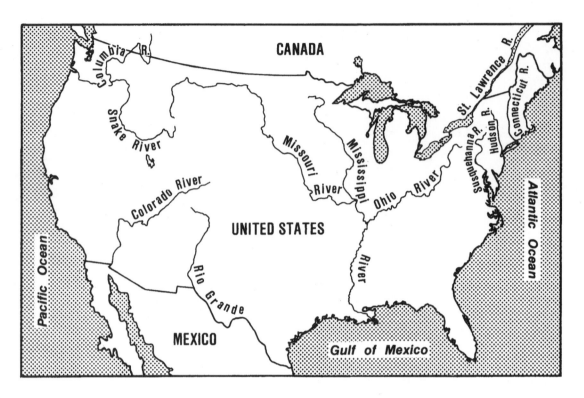

Water Systems in the United States

A Look at this map of the United States. Then follow the directions.

1.–5. One of the first geographic features you can see are the five large lakes in the north central region of the country. These are the Great Lakes. Their names, going from west to east, are (1) Lake Superior, (2) Lake Michigan, (3) Lake Huron, (4) Lake Erie, and (5) Lake Ontario. Write the number of each Great Lake on the map.

6. The Great Lakes are connected to the Atlantic Ocean by the Saint Lawrence River. Find the Saint Lawrence River on the map and write the number 6.

7. The largest river system in North America is located in the central United States. It is called the Mississippi River system. A *river system* is made up of a main river and all the other rivers that flow into it. These other rivers are called *tributaries*. Find the Mississippi River system on the map. Draw a line around it and label this river system number 7.

8. In the northwestern United States is another large river system. It is called the Columbia River system, named after the main river. Find the Columbia River system on your map. Draw a line around this river system, and then write the number 8 on it.

9. The Colorado River system is located in the southwestern United States. Draw a line around this river system and write the number 9 inside it.

10.–11. Most rivers in the United States eventually flow into one of two oceans—the Atlantic Ocean or the Pacific Ocean. The Atlantic Ocean borders the United States on the east. The Pacific Ocean borders the United States on the west. Find each ocean on your map. Write the number 10 on the Atlantic Ocean. Write the number 11 on the Pacific Ocean.

B Rivers have always been important to people. They have been used to water crops and as highways for travel. Sometimes, unfortunately, they have also been used as dumps for waste materials people want to get rid of. Answer the questions below.

1. Is there a river near where you live? _____

2. What is its name? _____

3. Into what ocean do its waters eventually flow? _____

   (If you live near one of the few rivers that does not flow into an ocean, find out where its water does go.)

4. What are some of the ways people have used rivers?

   _____

   _____

5. Is there a disadvantage in not having a river near a city? Why or why not?

   _____

   _____

   _____

Climate

When geographers use the word *weather,* they mean the daily changes in temperature, wind, cloudiness, and precipitation in a particular place. Remember, *precipitation* means snow, rain, sleet, or hail.

The word *climate* is also used by geographers. When geographers talk about the climate of a place, they mean the average or normal weather conditions of that place over a long time.

There are three main temperature zones on the earth: the tropics, the mid-latitudes, and the polar regions. The United States is located in the mid-latitude temperature zone. Temperatures in this zone change with the seasons.

Precipitation also varies from place to place on the earth's surface. There are three main precipitation zones: wet, dry, and wet-and-dry. Most places have different amounts of precipitation in different seasons. This means that they are wetter during one time of year and drier during another time of year. The United States has all three precipitation zones. Some parts of the United States are dry all of the time. We call these areas *deserts.* Some parts of the United States have wet and dry seasons. Other parts of the United States have precipitation all year long. There is no dry season or wet season.

You can tell what kind of climate a place has by looking at the temperature changes and the amount of precipitation over a long period of time.

	Climate Data											
	Jan.	Feb.	Mar.	Apr.	May	June	July	Aug.	Sept.	Oct.	Nov.	Dec.
HONOLULU, HAWAII												
Temperature (° F)	72.4	72.6	73.1	74.6	76.1	77.9	78.8	79.6	79.4	78.2	75.7	76.0
Precipitation (in.)	4.69	2.65	3.54	1.43	1.04	0.39	0.57	0.74	0.71	1.54	3.28	3.72
LEXINGTON, KY												
Temperature (° F)	33.5	35.1	43.7	54.2	64.1	72.8	76.2	74.9	69.1	57.6	44.7	36.0
Precipitation (in.)	4.17	3.24	4.52	3.63	3.80	4.17	4.40	3.35	2.79	2.31	3.14	3.60
ALBUQUERQUE, NM												
Temperature (° F)	34.6	39.5	46.2	54.9	63.8	73.2	77.1	75.1	68.4	54.8	43.9	35.1
Precipitation (in.)	0.36	0.35	0.41	0.56	0.63	0.59	1.44	1.31	0.91	0.80	0.42	0.46

The chart on page 32 shows the average temperatures and rainfalls in certain places. Study the temperatures and rainfalls for the three cities and answer the questions.

1. What city has a dry climate? _____

2. Which city has a wet and dry season? _____

    a. During which months does that city have a wet season?

    _____

    b. During which months does that city have a dry season?

    _____

3. Which city has about the same amount of precipitation all year long?_____

    _____

4. What does the word *weather* mean? _____

    _____

5. What does the word *climate* mean? _____

    _____

6. What are the three temperature zones on the earth?

    a. _____

    b. _____

    c. _____

7. In which temperature zone is most of the United States?

    _____

8. What are the three precipitation zones on the earth?

    a. _____

    b. _____

    c. _____

9. Which precipitation zones are found in the United States?

    _____

10. What is *precipitation?*

    _____

Natural Vegetation

Different kinds of plants grow in different parts of the United States. Have you ever wondered why this is so?

To answer the question, let's think of what makes plants grow. Plants need water, soil, and sunlight, and a certain number of days of warm, frost-free temperature. Different parts of the United States get different amounts of precipitation during the year. Different parts of the United States have different kinds of soil. Different parts of the United States get different amounts of sunlight. Finally, the number of frost-free days in the year varies in different parts of the United States.

A Answer the questions below.

1. What are the four things plants need in order to grow? _____

   _____

2. Do all parts of the United States have the same kind of soil, the same amount of sunlight and precipitation, and the same number of warm days?

   _____

Geographers have divided up the world into different natural environment regions. Four things go into making up a natural environment region. These four things are temperature, precipitation, soil, and vegetation. Look at the map of the world below.

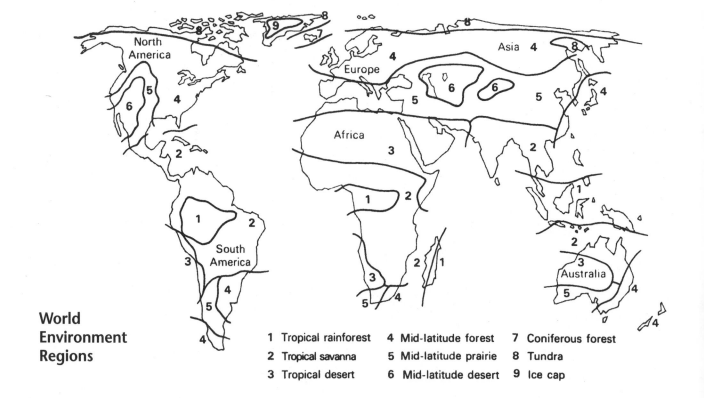

**World
Environment
Regions**

1 Tropical rainforest	4 Mid-latitude forest	7 Coniferous forest
2 Tropical savanna	5 Mid-latitude prairie	8 Tundra
3 Tropical desert	6 Mid-latitude desert	9 Ice cap

B Darken the area on the map on page 34 where the United States is found. (Don't forget to include Alaska!) What four natural environment regions are found in the United States?

a. _____   c. _____

b. _____   d. _____

C Now study the chart, which describes the natural vegetation in different regions. Which region on the chart best describes the area you live in?

Natural Environment Regions

Polar (Cold all year)	**9** Dry Polar (Ice cap) Some lichens, but no trees or grasses.	**8** Wet and Dry Polar (Tundra) Low-growing mosses, lichens, and dwarf woody plants. No trees.	**7** Wet Polar (Coniferous or cone-bearing forest) Needle-leaved evergreen trees, including fir, pine, and spruce.	
Mid-Latitude (Hot and cold seasons)	**6** Dry Mid-latitude (Desert) Scattered drought-resistant plants such as cactus.	**5** Wet and Dry Mid-latitude (Prairie) Continuous grass-cover; trees along course of streams.	**4** Wet Mid-latitude (Mid-latitude forest) Deciduous and/or evergreen trees.	colder ↑ ↓ warmer
Tropical (Hot all year)	**3** Dry Tropics (Desert) Scattered drought-resistant shrubs and grasses such as cactus.	**2** Wet and Dry Tropics (Savanna) Tropical grasslands with scattered trees.	**1** Wet Tropics (Tropical rain forest) Dense broadleaf evergreen trees.	
	wetter ⟶ ⟵ drier			

Population of the United States

The Bureau of the Census is the United States government agency that counts the number of people living in the country. In 1990, the Bureau of the Census estimated there were 249,632,692 people in the United States. The United States has the third largest population in the world. Only China and India have more people.

These 249,632,692 people are not spread evenly throughout the 50 states. More than half of them live in just nine states. Almost three-fourths of them live in just 20 states. Refer to the names of the states on the map on page 39.

Population Density Map

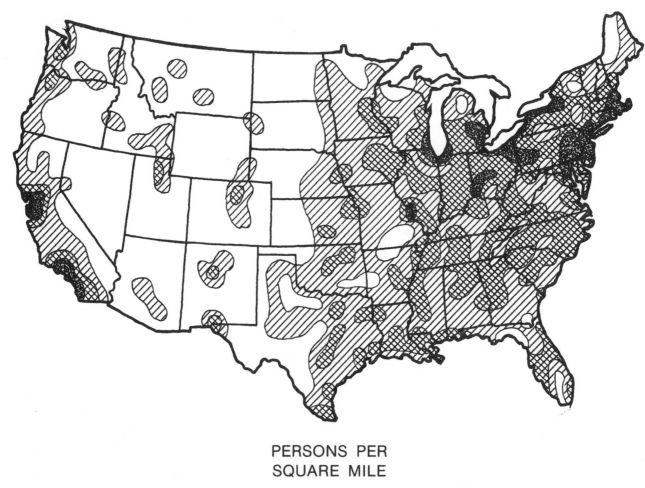

PERSONS PER
SQUARE MILE

Less Than 15	15 to 60	60 to 200	More Than 200

Study the map on page 36 and the chart on page 38; then answer the questions below.

1. Which nine states have the most people per square mile?

a. _____   f. _____

b. _____   g. _____

c. _____   h. _____

d. _____   i. _____

e. _____

2. List the remaining eleven states with large population densities.

a. _____   g. _____

b. _____   h. _____

c. _____   i. _____

d. _____   j. _____

e. _____   k. _____

f. _____

3. Is your state one of the 20 states with the most people?_____

4. California and New York are states with dense populations. What are some of the advantages that could encourage such large populations?

_____

_____

_____

_____

5. Maine, Nevada, and North Dakota do not have large populations. What are some reasons for such small populations?

_____

_____

_____

_____

UNIT 2

Geographers use the term *population density* to describe how many people live on each square mile of land. They say that there is "high population density" if many people live on each square mile of land. "Low population density" means that very few people live on each square mile of land.

The population density in the United States varies greatly from place to place. In cities, where many people live very close together in tall apartment buildings, population is very dense. In small towns, where most people live in separate houses with yards around them, population is less dense. In farm areas where one family may live on a very large farm, population density is very low.

The chart below lists the states in order of population density.

States in Order of Population Density (People per square mile)			
New Jersey	1,042	West Virginia	75
Rhode Island	960	Missouri	74
Massachusetts	768	Washington	73
Connecticut	678	Texas	65
Maryland	490	Vermont	61
New York	381	Minnesota	55
Delaware	342	Mississippi	55
Ohio	265	Iowa	50
Pennsylvania	265	Oklahoma	46
Florida	240	Arkansas	45
Illinois	206	Maine	40
California	191	Arizona	32
Hawaii	173	Colorado	32
Michigan	164	Kansas	30
Virginia	156	Oregon	30
Indiana	155	Nebraska	21
North Carolina	136	Utah	21
New Hampshire	124	New Mexico	13
Tennessee	118	Idaho	12
South Carolina	116	Nevada	11
Georgia	112	North Dakota	9
Louisiana	97	South Dakota	9
Kentucky	93	Montana	6
Wisconsin	90	Wyoming	5
Alabama	80	Alaska	1

Shade the 10 most densely populated states on the map. Then answer the questions below.

The United States

1. What does *population density* mean? _____

_____

2. If a state has a *low* population density, what does this mean?

_____

3. If a state has a *high* population density, what does this mean?

_____

4. Think of two reasons why a state might have a high population density.

   a. _____

   b. _____

5. Think of two reasons why a state might have a low population density.

   a. _____

   b. _____

6. Where does your state rank in population density? _____

Immigration

An *immigrant* is a person who moves to a new country from another country. The United States has been called a nation of immigrants. This is because the people of the United States have come to live here from many different places all over the world.

People have come to live in the United States for many different reasons. Some people have come to this country because here they might find better jobs. Some have come because there was no freedom where they used to live. Still others have come to the United States because of wars. Others have come to escape religious persecution.

When immigrants come to the United States, they bring with them the traditions of their own country. This great variety of traditions and people has helped make the United States a prosperous and exciting country.

In the 1980 census, many people identified the country from which they, their parents, or their ancestors came. The maps below show how some ethnic groups are concentrated in the United States. Each shaded state has at least 500,000 persons of the indicated ethnic group.

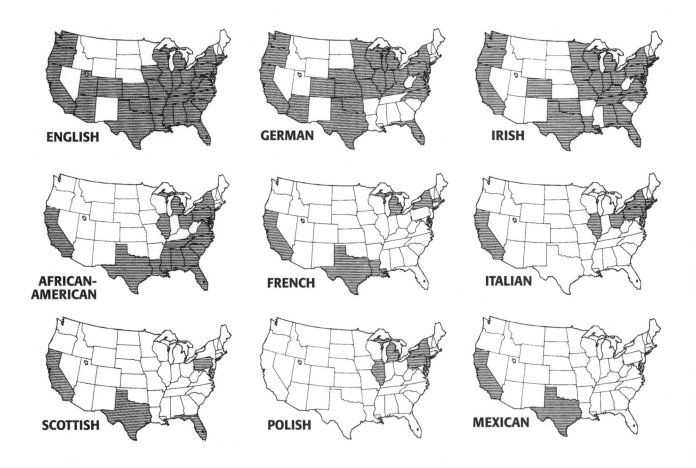

ENGLISH   GERMAN   IRISH

AFRICAN-AMERICAN   FRENCH   ITALIAN

SCOTTISH   POLISH   MEXICAN

Answer the questions below.

1. List four reasons why people from other countries have come to live in the United States.

   a. _____

   b. _____

   c. _____

   d. _____

2. Who is an *immigrant?* _____

   _____

3. Why is the United States sometimes called a nation of immigrants? _____

   _____

4. According to the maps, which ethnic group has large numbers in the most states?

   _____

5. Which two states have great numbers of people of Mexican descent?

   _____

6. In which part of the United States do the largest numbers of people of Polish descent live?

   _____

7. List three states that are shaded for seven ethnic groups.

   _____

8. List three states that are not shaded for any group.

   _____

9. What might a newcomer to the United States look for when choosing a place to live?

   _____

10. If you were immigrating to the United States, what would you most want to have in the city or town you choose to live in?

   _____

   _____

In the 1990 census, many people again indicated the country from which they, their parents, or their ancestors came.

The chart below shows the 15 largest ancestry groups in the United States, according to the 1990 census.

German	57,900,000
Irish	38,700,000
English	32,700,000
African-American	23,800,000
Italian	14,700,000
Mexican	11,600,000
French	10,300,000
Polish	9,400,000
American Indian	8,700,000
Dutch	6,200,000
Russian	3,000,000
Puerto Rican	1,900,000
Chinese	1,500,000
Filipino	1,400,000
Japanese	1,000,000

Study the chart and then answer the questions below.

1. How many groups are included? _____

2. Which ethnic group has about 10 million members? _____

3. Which group has one million members? _____

4. Which group has the most members? _____

5. How many people are of Chinese descent? _____

6. How many people are of Italian descent? _____

7. How many more people are of German descent than of Irish descent? _____

8. Which group has more members—American Indian or African-American? _____

9. List all the groups that have over 20 million members.

    _____

    _____

10. Which group has more members—Mexican or Puerto Rican? _____

Settling the Wilderness of Tennessee

Americans from the early colonies crossed the Appalachian Mountains in North Carolina in the 1780s. They went by boat down the Cumberland River to the middle of what is now the state of Tennessee. They went there to build new homes.

When they first came to Tennessee, there were dense forests. There was no cleared land to farm. There were no roads and no towns. These early settlers had to cut down trees to clear land for farms. They had to clear paths through the forests to make roads. They built houses out of logs.

After several years, the land had changed. Now a small town called Nashville stood where there had once been only dense forests. These settlers had changed the way the land looked. They had changed their geographic environment.

Answer the questions below.

1. Where did the settlers in the story come from? _____

   _____

2. In what present-day state did they build their settlement?

   _____

3. What was the land like before the settlers came?

   _____

   _____

4. Name three ways the settlers changed the land.

   a. _____

   _____

   b. _____

   _____

   c. _____

   _____

5. What does *geographic environment* mean? _____

   _____

   _____

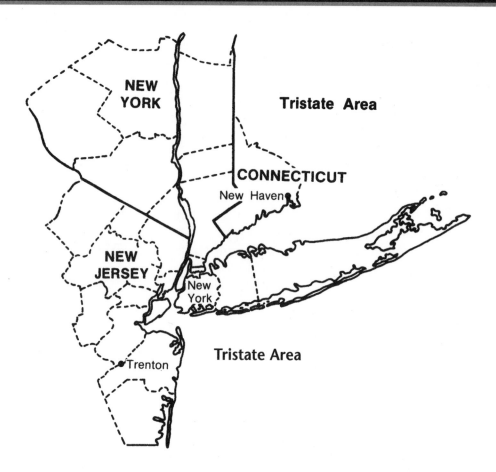
Planning for Parks

Many people live in the counties surrounding New York City. Builders are putting up new houses, new factories, and new shopping centers all the time. Many people in this area are afraid that soon there will be no more open land. They want to set aside land for hiking trails, bicycle paths, and parks.

The Regional Plan Association is starting a campaign to buy land in the area. They are looking for land from Trenton, New Jersey, to New Haven, Connecticut. They are even looking for open land in New York City.

Planners think that parks will make life better for people living in the counties around New York City. They want city and town governments to buy land for parks for people to use.

People could use parks for picnics and boating. There could be trails for horseback riders and playgrounds for children. In some places, plays and concerts are held in the parks. Parks do make life better for people.

■ Answer the questions below.

1. What are many people in the counties surrounding New York City worried about?

_____

2. For what purpose was the Regional Plan Association started?

_____

_____

3. What three states surround New York City?

  a. _____

  b. _____

  c. _____

4. Between what two cities are planners looking for open land?

_____

5. Why do people want their cities to buy open land?

_____

_____

6. Are there parks in your city or town? Where are they?

_____

_____

7. How can money be provided for a town to buy more land for parks?

_____

_____

8. List three ways that people can use parks in their cities.

  a. _____

  b. _____

  c. _____

Acid Rain and the Environment

There's an old saying: "What goes up must come down." Americans in many parts of the country have been finding out how true this saying is. They are finding that the fish in their lakes are dying off. They are finding that pine trees in their forests are losing their green foliage.

Scientists think that the cause of destruction is *acid rain*. Acid rain comes from pollution in the air. The pollution is in the smoke from industries and from car exhausts. The smoke comes from hundreds of smokestacks in the industrialized areas of our country. It rises into the upper atmosphere, where the winds carry it hundreds of miles from the factories. Eventually, the pollutants in the smoke mix with rain to form acid rain. When this acid rain falls to the ground, it harms plants and pollutes the groundwater. In many areas of the Northeast, lakes that once were excellent for fishing now have few fish.

There are many questions about acid rain that need to be answered. Who will pay for the cleanup of pollution? Should the industries that caused the problem pay? Should the people who live in the areas harmed by the acid rain contribute? Should the federal government spend taxes to deal with pollution? Should the customers of businesses and the drivers of cars pay? Cleaning up pollution is not an easy task, but most Americans today think it is very important to take better care of our environment.

Acid Rain: The Sources

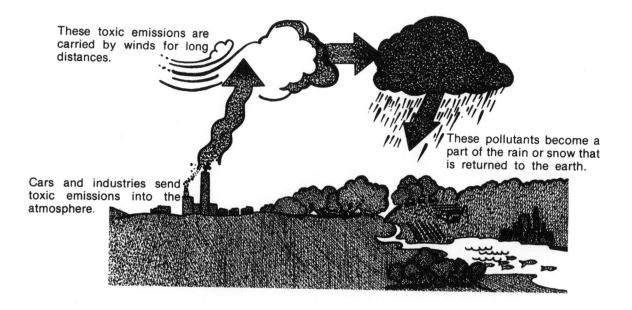

These toxic emissions are carried by winds for long distances.

These pollutants become a part of the rain or snow that is returned to the earth.

Cars and industries send toxic emissions into the atmosphere.

■ Study the map and answer the questions.

1. In what parts of the United States is acid rain a big problem?

_____

2. According to the map, which four states are most heavily affected by acid rain?

   a. _____

   b. _____

   c. _____

   d. _____

3. According to the map, what other states are affected by acid rain?

_____

_____

4. What are two possible causes of acid rain?

   a. _____

   b. _____

Acid Rain: The Fallout

Acid Rain

5. What makes acid rain spread over such a big area?

_____

_____

6. What harm to the environment does acid rain cause? _____

_____

_____

7. According to the map, what other country besides the United States has a problem with acid rain?

_____

_____

8. How can money be raised to eliminate the acid rain problem?

_____

_____

Water for the Arizona Desert

Americans are constantly changing their geographic environment. Much of the state of Arizona is desert. There is very little rainfall there. More people moved into the state. These new Arizona citizens needed water.

The Central Arizona Project was a plan to bring water from the Colorado River to the city of Phoenix. When it was completed, the project carried water for 330 miles. It pumped the water 1,200 feet uphill. Dams were built on smaller rivers, called *tributaries*. Behind these dams, big lakes were created to store the water.

Now that the project is completed, the land has changed. The new water supply means that even more people can live in central Arizona. The new people will have water for their houses. New businesses can be built because there is a water supply. Land that was once a desert can be used for farmland.

Answer the questions below.

1. What kind of geographic environment is found in much of Arizona?

   _____

2. Why was the Central Arizona Project built? _____

   _____

3. Where does the water have to be carried from? _____

   _____

4. How many miles does the water have to be carried? _____

5. Name three ways that central Arizona has changed since the project was completed.

   a. _____

   b. _____

   c. _____

6. Who in Arizona do you think might have supported the project and why?

   _____

   _____

   _____

7. What is a *tributary?* _____

   _____

Railroads in the United States

The roads, railroads, waterways, and airways over which people move their goods are called *transportation arteries*. The money that people earn in part depends on these transportation arteries. In this unit, we are going to look at four types of transportation arteries and learn why they are so important to people in the United States.

Railroads carry almost as much freight as trucks and barges. They carry mostly bulk goods such as coal, wheat, and very large equipment. There are many reasons why railroads are cheaper to use than trucks. One reason is that they don't use as much fuel to carry goods as trucks do.

 Study the map of the U.S. rail systems below and answer the questions.

Railroad Freight Traffic in the United States

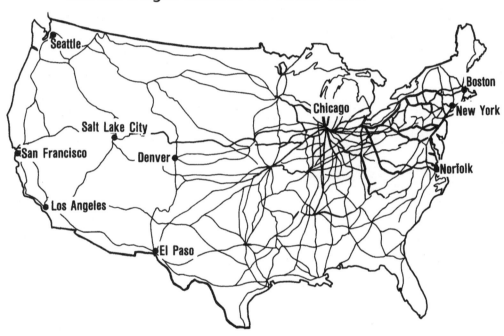

1. Where is the greatest concentration of railroad freight traffic?

   _____

2. If you were shipping freight from Seattle to Los Angeles,
   what major city would it pass through?

   _____

3. Why might a business ship by railroad rather than by truck?

   _____

4. Is there a major freight railroad near where you live?_____

The Saint Lawrence Seaway Lesson 2

UNIT 4

The Great Lakes are connected to the Atlantic Ocean by the Saint Lawrence River. Today large ocean-going ships can sail all the way to the westernmost point on Lake Superior. This is because a series of *locks* has been built. Locks are used to raise and lower boats on waterways. These locks make it possible for ships to sail around the waterfalls and rapids on the rivers and between the lakes.

A Study the map of the St. Lawrence-Great Lakes Waterway below and answer the questions.

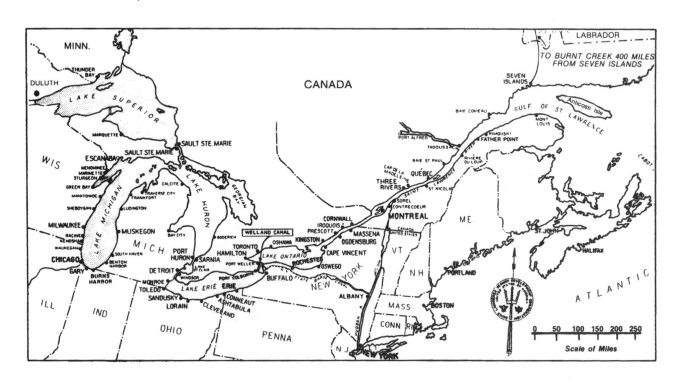

St. Lawrence-Great Lakes Waterway

1. Name the bodies of water that a ship would cross in sailing from Father Point (near the Gulf of St. Lawrence on the eastern side of the map) to Duluth.

   a. _____ River

   b. Lake _____

   c. _____ Canal

   d. Lake _____

   e. Lake _____

   f. Lake _____

   g. Lake _____

2. About how far is it from Duluth at the western end of Lake Superior to the Atlantic Ocean?

_____

3. Name the states that border the Great Lakes, from west to east.

a. _____   e. _____

b. _____   f. _____

c. _____   g. _____

d. _____   h. _____

4. What country borders the St. Lawrence-Great Lakes Seaway to the north?

_____

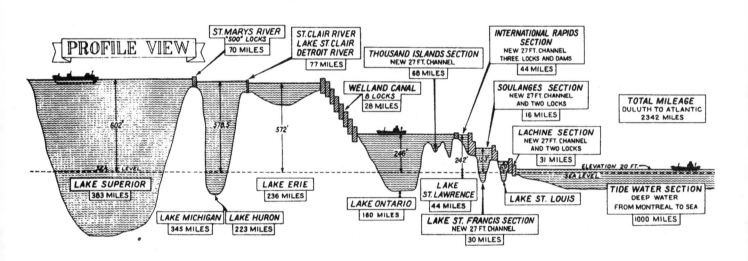

B Study the profile view of the Seaway and answer the questions below.

1. How far above sea level is Lake Superior? _____

2. How many locks are there in the Welland Canal section of the Seaway? _____

3. Why are there so many locks at this particular place?

_____

_____

4. How many locks are there between Lake Ontario and the Tide Water Section?

_____

_____

United States Highways

The United States has three-and-a-half million miles of surfaced roads. People use these roads every day to go to work, stores, or school. These roads are built by government highway departments. Local towns and cities, counties, and states build some of the roads. The federal government builds many roads, too.

The map below shows one of the highway networks built by the United States government. This network is called the Interstate Highway System. It is possible to travel on the interstate highways from coast to coast without ever having to stop at a traffic light! The interstate highways have several lanes of traffic going in each direction. Cars, trucks, and buses can move at high speeds on these highways.

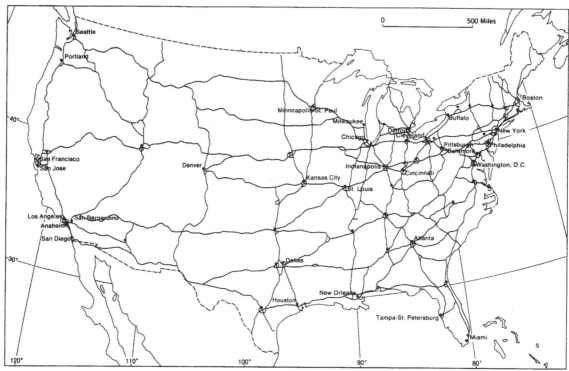

United States Interstate Highway System

Answer the questions.

1. What is the title of the map? _____

2. Approximately how many miles is it from Denver to St. Louis? _____

3. What interstate highway is closest to your home?_____

4. Who builds the Interstate Highway System in the United States?_____

5. If you were driving from Houston to Washington, D.C., on interstate highways, what major cities would you pass through?

_____

Air Transportation in the United States

Today most travel between cities in the United States is by airplane. Every day millions of people travel by air.

What makes air travel so popular? It is the fastest way to travel long distances. Flying time from New York to Chicago is less than two hours. It would take at least eight times that amount of time to drive from New York to Chicago! Air fares have become less expensive, too. As airlines compete with each other for customers, they offer special low fares. More and more people are able to afford to fly.

Many cities want an airport. Airports make distant cities easier to reach. Businesses will move into a city with an airport. That would create more jobs for the people who live in that city.

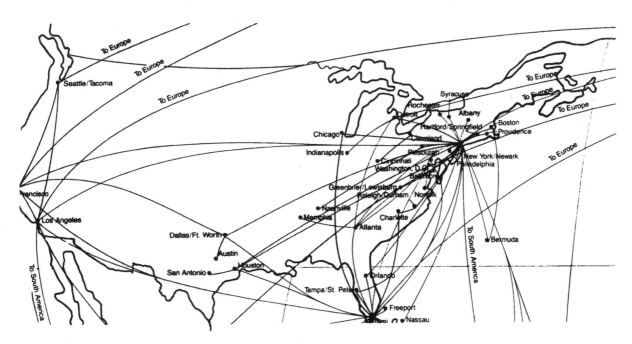

Airline Routes Across the United States

Answer the questions below.

1. How do most people travel between cities today? _____

2. List two reasons why millions of people are traveling by air.

   _____

   _____

3. Why might a city want to have an airport?_____

   _____

4. Are there any major airports in or near your hometown? _____

Communication Links in the Past

The United States is a very big country. Before the days of fast communication by telephone and radio, it took many days to get a message from one part of the country to another. As Americans moved to the West, they wanted ways to send fast messages to their families and friends they left behind.

In 1860, William Russell came up with an idea. He set up a pony express mail service. He built 190 stations, each ten to fifteen miles apart, from St. Joseph, Missouri, to San Francisco, California. A man rode a horse at top speed. At the next station, he changed horses and rode at top speed to the next station. After 75 miles, another rider took over. Russell was able to get a letter from Missouri to California in 10 days! But the pony express lasted only 18 months. In 1861, the overland telegraph was completed.

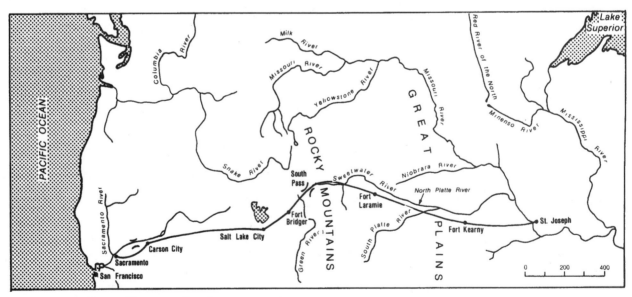

Pony Express Route

Study the map on page 54 and answer the following questions.

1. Why did it take so long to send a message across the United States before the invention of the telegraph and the telephone?

   _____

   _____

2. How did William Russell solve this communication problem?

   _____

3. How far apart were the pony express stations?

   _____

4. How many miles did each rider travel? _____

5. Look at the map on page 54.

   a. What city marks the starting point of the pony express service?_____

   b. In what city did it end? _____

6. About how many miles long was the pony express route?

   _____

7. Write the names of the landforms, from east to west, that the pony express route crossed.

   _____

   _____

8. What difficulties might these landforms cause for the pony express riders?

   _____

   _____

9. Why was the pony express considered to be fast communication?

   _____

   _____

10. List three other more recent types of fast communication.

    _____

    _____

    _____

Communications in the United States Today

Imagine being able to talk to anyone anywhere in the world. Imagine talking in English and instantly having your message translated into any language and delivered in minutes to its destination. Imagine being able to see and talk to three people in three different cities at the same time. Communication experts tell us that soon all of these kinds of conversations will happen all the time.

Today instant communication anywhere in the United States occurs by means of satellite links. Businesses all over the United States use satellite communications to talk to their customers faster.

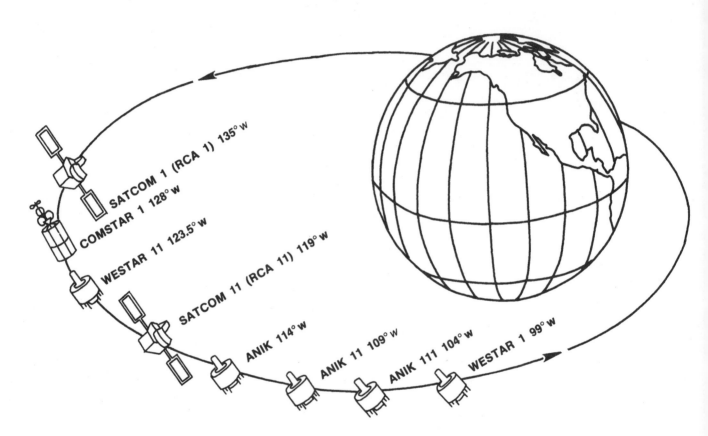

Orbit Satellites in North America

People who live in places that are hard to reach with ground communications often had a difficult time talking to others. Now satellite communications make it possible for them to reach other people quickly. If an emergency happens, they will be able to get help in a hurry.

Ground telephone connections have also been improved. Strands of glass as thin as a human hair are used to carry messages from city to city in the Northeast. A cable of these glass strands may be only a half-inch thick. Yet this cable can carry hundreds of thousands of conversations at the same time, which is many, many more conversations than a copper cable thick as a wrist can carry. The glass strands are less expensive to make. A mile-long thread of glass can be made from a tablespoon of raw material!

■ Answer the questions below.

1. What are three kinds of conversations that will happen all the time in the future?

   a. _____

   b. _____

   c. _____

2. How do satellite links help businesses? _____

_____

3. How have satellite links improved the lives of people who live in places far away from other people?

_____

_____

4. Who else might be helped by satellite links? _____

_____

_____

5. What kind of material is now used to carry ground communication messages?

_____

_____

6. List two reasons why this material is better than the copper cable that has been used in the past.

   a. _____

   b. _____

The Port of New York City was once the number one port in the nation. Today, however, New York City is just one of many important national ports. What has caused this change?

New York's number one position changed when the way ship cargo was loaded changed. Many years ago, the cargo was brought to or taken away from the docks by railroads. The cargo was loaded or unloaded piece by piece onto or off of ships. It took many workers, called *longshoremen*, many hours to load or unload a ship. The docks in New York City were crowded with longshoremen.

Today cargo is loaded onto ships in huge *containers*. The cargo is brought to the docks on large trucks. Two things are needed for a container port to be successful. First, these trucks need space to load and unload the giant containers. Second, the highways connecting the port to other big cities have to be fast and easy to reach.

New York City did not have enough space for these big trucks. Also, the interstate highway connections from the New York City loading docks to other cities were not easy to reach. Therefore, the new container port was built across the Hudson River at Newark, New Jersey, where there was plenty of space and excellent interstate highways leading right to the port area.

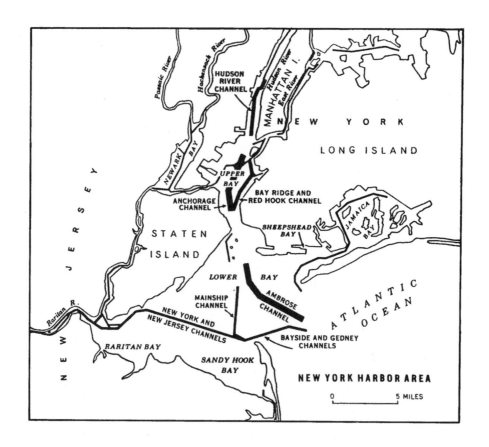

Today most of the container-loading docks for the New York area are located in New Jersey at Port Newark-Elizabeth. In 1962, most of the port's business was on the New York City side of the port. Practically no cargo was containerized. Today 90% of all cargo is containerized, and most of the New York area's shipping business takes place at Newark-Elizabeth, which is known as "America's container capital."

Study the map on page 58 and answer the following questions.

1. In the past 30 years, what change has taken place in the way ships are loaded?

_____

_____

2. What is a containerized port? _____

_____

3. What two things are necessary to have a successful containerized port?

 a. _____

 b. _____

4. Why was the New York City side of the port not a good place for a containerized port?

_____

5. What made Newark-Elizabeth an ideal place to build a containerized port?

_____

_____

6. What has happened to the amount of cargo handled in the New York City part of the port since 1962?

_____

7. What has happened to the amount of cargo handled in the Newark-Elizabeth part of the port since 1962?

_____

8. Why is the Newark-Elizabeth port area known as "America's container capital"?

_____

_____

In September 1972, a new transportation system opened up in the San Francisco Bay area. It is called *BART,* which stands for Bay Area Rapid Transit. The BART system connects the towns on the eastern side of San Francisco Bay with the city of San Francisco on the western side of the bay. The transit system forms a giant X across the bay area.

People can travel quickly and inexpensively from one town to another. BART trains run at speeds of up to 80 miles per hour between stations. The trains are started, accelerated, slowed, and stopped by computerized instructions. An attendant rides in the front cab of the train. However, he or she has nothing to do except when there's an emergency.

BART trains run at 6-minute intervals during the rush hours. At other times during the day and evening, the trains run every 12 to 20 minutes. Passengers purchase magnetically coded tickets at ticket machines. These machines even make change for the customer. Fares are moderate, averaging about $3.00 for a trip.

The builders of BART hoped that commuters in the bay area would use this fast and less expensive transportation system instead of their cars. They hoped that traffic on the highways in the bay area would decrease as more people used BART.

Answer these questions below.

1. What does BART stand for?

   _____

2. Why is BART called a rapid transit system?

   _____

   _____

3. How fast do BART trains run? _____

4. How often do BART trains run? _____

5. How much does it cost, on the average, to ride on BART?

   _____

6. What did the builders of BART hope would happen to car traffic in San Francisco after people started riding on BART?

   _____

   _____

7. What features of BART might make people want to ride on it to get to work?

_____

_____

8. Why might some people <u>not</u> want to ride on the BART trains?

_____

_____

9. The map at the right shows how many minutes it takes to travel from the Oakland City Center and from the Embarcadero to various stations on the BART system.

a. Circle the Oakland City Center station on the map.

b. Circle the Embarcadero station on the map.

c. How many minutes does it take to travel from the Oakland City station to:

Concord? _____

Fremont? _____

across the bay to the Embarcadero?

_____

d. How many minutes does it take to travel from the Embarcadero station to:

Daly City?_____

the Civic Center? _____

10. What kind of public transportation is available to people in your area?

_____

_____

_____

_____

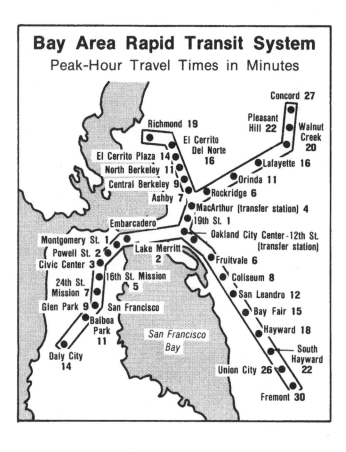

Bay Area Rapid Transit System
Peak-Hour Travel Times in Minutes

Concord 27
Pleasant Hill 22
Walnut Creek 20
Richmond 19
El Cerrito Del Norte 16
El Cerrito Plaza 14
Lafayette 16
North Berkeley 11
Orinda 11
Central Berkeley 9
Rockridge 6
Ashby 7
MacArthur (transfer station) 4
Embarcadero
19th St. 1
Oakland City Center - 12th St. (transfer station)
Montgomery St. 1
Lake Merritt 2
Powell St. 2
Civic Center 3
Fruitvale 6
24th St. Mission 7
16th St. Mission 5
Coliseum 8
Glen Park 9
San Leandro 12
San Francisco
Bay Fair 15
Balboa Park 11
Hayward 18
San Francisco Bay
South Hayward 22
Daly City 14
Union City 26
Fremont 30

To a geographer a *region* is an area with a lot of features that are alike or similar. There are all kinds of regions. Physical geographers are interested in areas where the land features are alike. They talk about the Atlantic Coastal Plain, the Great Basin, or the Rocky Mountains. They talk about river systems.

Cultural geographers are interested in areas where the people are alike or similar in some ways. For example, they talk about regions where many people from one country have made their homes. They talk about regions where people share a common language or a common religion. They may use the term *Chinatown* when talking about many U.S. cities to describe a region in a city where many Americans of Chinese descent have made their homes.

Economic geographers are interested in areas where people earn their living in similar ways. They talk about regions like the Cotton Belt and the Wheat Belt where many farmers raise cotton or wheat. They talk about regions where certain types of industries are located. The term *Rust Belt* is sometimes used to refer to an area of the United States where older manufacturing industries are dying out.

Political geographers are interested in areas where governments are similar. A political map of the United States, for example, shows the states. Political geographers are interested in studying voting patterns. They want to find out, for example, what parts of the United States tend to vote for a particular political party.

A Answer the following questions.

1. List four types of geographers.

   _____

   _____

2. What does the term *Rust Belt* refer to?

   _____

   _____

B Answer these questions by circling the letter of the correct answer.

1. The word *region* means
   a. an area where things are alike.
   b. an area where things are different.
   c. your residence.

2. An example of a physical region is
   a. Little Italy.
   b. the Cotton Belt.
   c. the Great Plains.

3. An example of a cultural region is
   a. the Rocky Mountains.
   b. Midwest voters.
   c. an Irish neighborhood.

4. An example of an economic region is
   a. the automobile production area.
   b. the Great Lakes region.
   c. New England voters.

5. An example of a political region is
   a. the Amish settlement in Pennsylvania.
   b. the Mississippi River.
   c. the northeastern big city voters.

6. Cultural geographers study
   a. big city traffic patterns.
   b. people's common language and religion.
   c. how people earn their living.

7. Economic geographers study
   a. where and how people earn their living.
   b. how many different places of worship are in the area.
   c. the Ohio River.

8. Political geographers study
   a. ways people earn a living.
   b. people's voting patterns.
   c. the landforms of an area.

9. Physical geographers study
   a. the voting patterns of the people.
   b. the ways people live.
   c. areas where the land features are alike.

10. Geography is the study
    a. of people you know.
    b. of the earth and its resources.
    c. of animals and plants.

New England

Six states make up the geographic region known as New England. These states are Maine, New Hampshire, Vermont, Massachusetts, Rhode Island, and Connecticut. The early settlers farmed this rocky, hilly land. Only a few of today's New Englanders farm, however. Most of the 13 million people who live in these states work in industries producing computers, machine tools, airplane engines, and precision instruments. They live in or near the region's large cities like Boston, Hartford, Providence, and Springfield.

Many tourists come to visit New England each year. The region is famous for the beautiful colors of the trees in the fall. New England also has many famous historic places. One is the village at Plymouth, Massachusetts, where the Pilgrims first settled.

New England Region

A Darken the six New England states on the map of the United States.

The United States

B Answer the questions.

1. What is the population of New England? _____

2. What did New England's first settlers do for a living? _____

3. What do most New Englanders today do for a living?

   _____

4. Name two reasons why people come to New England to visit.

   _____

5. Why do you think only a few people in new England still farm?

   _____

6. List the New England states from the one farthest south to the one farthest north.

   a. _____   d. _____

   b. _____   e. _____

   c. _____   f. _____

C Match the city in Column A with its state in Column B. Write the letter from Column B in the blank.

Column A	Column B
_____ 1. Boston	a. Connecticut
_____ 2. Hartford	b. Maine
_____ 3. Montpelier	c. Massachusetts
_____ 4. Portland	d. Vermont
_____ 5. Providence	e. New Hampshire
_____ 6. Concord	f. Rhode Island
_____ 7. Augusta	
_____ 8. Springfield	
_____ 9. Burlington	

U N I T 5

Seven states make up the Middle Atlantic region. These states are New York, New Jersey, Pennsylvania, Delaware, Maryland, Virginia, and West Virginia.

The Middle Atlantic region is divided in half. In the western half are the Appalachian Mountains with their coal mines and steel mills. In the eastern half are many of the region's big cities. It is often called the *gateway* region due to the many seaports there. The nation's largest city, New York City, with more than seven million people, is in the Middle Atlantic region. Philadelphia, Baltimore, Richmond, Trenton, Wilmington, and Newark are other large cities in this region.

The capital of the United States, Washington, D.C., is located in the Middle Atlantic region. The President of the United States, the Congress, and the military services all have their headquarters in Washington, D.C.

Its many cities make the Middle Atlantic region the most *urbanized* part of the United States. A solid string of cities stretches almost all the way from Richmond in Virginia north to Boston in Massachusetts. This string of cities is sometimes called a *megalopolis,* meaning "giant city."

The people who live in these cities need food to eat. Beyond the cities are many dairy farms, which produce milk for the cities. There are also *truck farms,* which produce fresh vegetables and fruits for city food stores.

Middle Atlantic Region

■ Answer the questions.

1. The Middle Atlantic region is the most urbanized region in the United States.

   What does *urbanized* mean? _____

2. About how many people live in New York City? _____

3. After each state below, write the name of a city that is located within that state.

   a. New York _____   **e.** Maryland _____

   b. Pennsylvania _____   **f.** West Virginia _____

   c. New Jersey _____   **g.** Virginia _____

   d. Delaware _____

4. What does the word *megalopolis* mean? _____

5. Why are there many farms in the Middle Atlantic region?_____

   _____

6. What two types of farms can be found in this region?_____

   _____

7. What two states does Washington, D. C., border on? _____

8. What two Middle Atlantic states border on a Great Lake?_____

9. Darken the seven Middle Atlantic states on the map of the United States.

The United States

Southeast Region

The seven states in the Southeast region of the United States are North Carolina, Tennessee, South Carolina, Georgia, Alabama, Mississippi, and Florida. More than 40 million people live in these seven states.

The Southeast region was once the center of the Confederate States of America, the states that left the United States in 1861 and fought the Civil War with the Union. In 1861, the Southeast region was mostly a region of farms. These farms produced cotton, tobacco, and sugar cane. Today, there are still many farms in the region. Forests cover 60% of the region. From these southeastern forests workers produce furniture, building materials, and much of the pulpwood used in making paper.

The Southeast region is not just a region of farms and forests, however. Many industries have moved into the region. The textile and food-processing industries have built many factories throughout the Southeast region.

Florida is famous for its warm climate in the winter. Americans from all over the United States come to this state for vacations. In fact, millions of vacationers come to all parts of this region every year, bringing billions of dollars into these seven states. *Tourism* is a major industry in the Southeast region.

Southeast Region

■ Answer the questions below.

1. What famous event in American history took place mostly in the Southeast

   region beginning in 1861?_____

2. How did most people in the Southeast region in 1861 earn a living?_____

3. What were the Confederate States of America? _____

   _____

4. What kinds of industries can you find today in the Southeast region?

   _____

5. How much of the land in the Southeast region is forest?_____

6. What are three products that people in the Southeast region make from trees?

   _____

7. What influence do you think the growing of cotton and the textile industry might
   have on one another?

   _____

8. What does *tourism* mean? _____

   _____

9. Why do you think tourism is such an important industry in Florida?

   _____

10. Darken the seven states of the Southeast region on the map on this page.

11. List the capitals of these seven states.

_____

_____

_____

_____

_____

_____

_____

The United States

UNIT 5

There are six states in the Great Lakes region. These six states are Wisconsin, Michigan, Illinois, Indiana, Ohio, and Kentucky. The five Great Lakes are the world's largest body of fresh water. The lakes are important for shipping. These lakes are also used by the people in this region for *recreation*. The people use the lakes for swimming, boating, and fishing.

The Great Lakes region is famous as the center of American industry. Most American steel and American cars are manufactured there. These industries are located in this region because of the good transportation on the Great Lakes. There are also large amounts of iron and coal nearby. The steel industry depends on iron and coal.

Some of the region's large cities are Chicago, Cleveland, Detroit, Milwaukee, Toledo, Cincinnati, and Louisville.

The Great Lakes region is also famous for its farmlands. The summers are hot, and there is plenty of rainfall. The soil is very fertile. Huge crops of corn and soybeans grow there on some of the best farmland in the world. Wisconsin in the nation's Dairy Belt produces more milk, butter, and cheese than any other state.

Great Lakes Region

■ Answer the following questions.

1. Label each of the five Great Lakes on the map below.

2. List three ways in which the people of the region use the Great Lakes.

   _____

   _____

3. List two important industries in the Great Lakes region.

   _____

4. What are two important crops grown in the Great Lakes region?

   _____

5. Why is Wisconsin part of the Dairy Belt? _____

   _____

6. What makes this region so good for farming? _____

   _____

7. List three important cities in this region.

   _____

8. What is the most southern Great Lakes region state? _____

9. What is the most northern Great Lakes region state? _____

10. Which state in the region does not border on a Great Lake? _____

11. Darken the six states of the Great Lakes region on the map below.

The United States

South Central Region

There are four states in the South Central region of the United States. These states are Texas, Oklahoma, Arkansas, and Louisiana. Two geographic features helped shape this region: the Mississippi River and the large amounts of oil found underground.

The Mississippi River forms the eastern boundary of the South Central region. The Mississippi and its *tributaries* form the third largest river system in the world. The Mississippi River system covers 31 states and stretches from the Rocky Mountains on the west to the Appalachian Mountains on the east. To control flooding along the Mississippi, the Army Corps of Engineers has built levees along the river's edges. A *levee* is a high wall that helps keep the river's waters from flooding the surrounding land.

Oil was first discovered in the South Central region near Beaumont, Texas, in 1901. Soon oil deposits beneath Oklahoma, Louisiana, and other parts of Texas were being tapped. Many people in the South Central region have jobs connected to the oil industry. Some people work on *offshore oil rigs* in the Gulf of Mexico. Others drill for oil on land. Still others work at oil refineries. Petrochemical industry workers make products such as plastics as a byproduct of oil or *petroleum.*

Another big industry in the South Central region is farming and ranching. In the western part of the region, there is not much rainfall. Farmers depend on *irrigation* to water their fields. Pumped from deep underground wells, this water cannot be replaced quickly. Therefore, farmers in this region are trying to produce crops that will not need as much water.

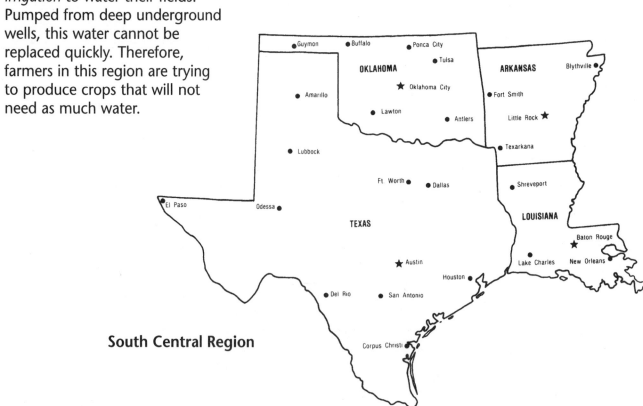

South Central Region

■ Study the map on page 72 and answer these questions.

1. Label the Gulf of Mexico and the Mississippi River on the map below.

2. How many states does the Mississippi River system cover? _____

3. How many river systems in the world are larger than the Mississippi River system?_____

4. Why has the Army Corps of Engineers built dams along the Mississippi River?

_____

5. When was oil discovered in Texas? _____

6. List three jobs related to the oil industry. _____

_____

7. What might happen to many people in the South Central region if the supply
   of oil there ran out?

_____

8. Why are farmers in the South Central region trying to produce crops
   that don't need as much water to grow?

_____

9. What states border the part of Oklahoma that is called "the panhandle"? _____

_____

10. Darken the four states of the South Central region on the map below.

The United States

North Central Region

There are seven states in the North Central region. These states are North Dakota, South Dakota, Minnesota, Iowa, Nebraska, Kansas, and Missouri. These states are sometimes called the "breadbasket of the world." That is because much of the world's *grain* crops are grown there. This region has many very large farms. Farmers grow crops such as corn, wheat, oats, and soybeans.

Transportation is very important in the North Central region. Many of these large farms are far from city markets. The farmers depend on the railroad and on the interstate highways to get their crops to the cities.

Only 17.5 million people live in this area. That is about the same number of people that New York state has. But the North Central region is almost 10 times the size of New York state! Geographers say that the region has a *low population density.* This means that there are not many people living on each square mile of land.

Many of the cities in the North Central region started as market centers for the farmers. *Agribusiness* is still important today, but new industries are also moving into these cities. Both St. Louis, Missouri, and Wichita, Kansas, are major aircraft centers. Minneapolis, Minnesota, and Omaha, Nebraska, are important banking centers.

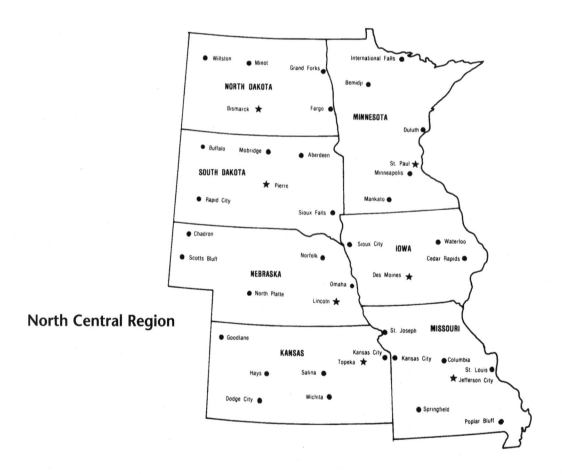

North Central Region

■ Answer the following questions.

1. Why is the North Central region sometimes called "the breadbasket of the world"?

_____

2. List three important grain crops grown in the North Central region.

_____

3. List three important cities in the North Central region.

_____

4. Why are railroads and interstate highways so important to farmers
   in the North Central region?

_____

5. What does *population density* mean? _____

_____

6. Are the states in the North Central region densely populated? Why or why not?

_____

7. What North Central state borders on a Great Lake? _____

8. List four cities that are developing industries other than agribusiness.
   What new industries are moving into these areas?

_____

_____

9. Darken the seven states of the North Central region on the map below.

The United States

Four Corners Region

There are four states in the Four Corners region of the United States. These four states are Utah, Colorado, Arizona, and New Mexico. The region is called the Four Corners because four corners of the states meet at one point. It is the only place in the United States where a person can stand in four states at the same time.

The Four Corners region is an area of high mountains and vast deserts. The Rocky Mountains sometimes reach heights of over 14,000 feet.

Much of the land in the Four Corners region belongs to the federal government. About 70% of Utah, 44% of Arizona, 36% of Colorado, and 33% of New Mexico are U.S. government property. Some of America's most beautiful national parks are in these four states. Grand Canyon, Rocky Mountain, Carlsbad Caverns, and Zion National Parks are in the Four Corners Region. Each year millions of Americans visit these and other national parks.

There are also many Indian reservations in the Four Corners region. The Navajo reservation, for example, covers an area about one-third the size of the New England states! On the reservations, many families live as their ancestors lived. They raise sheep, weave rugs, and make beautiful silver jewelry.

The warm, dry climate of the region makes it an attractive home to many Americans. As the population grows, however, more water must be found. The water for many of the region's cities is brought in from great distances. Denver's water is brought across the Rocky Mountains from western Colorado.

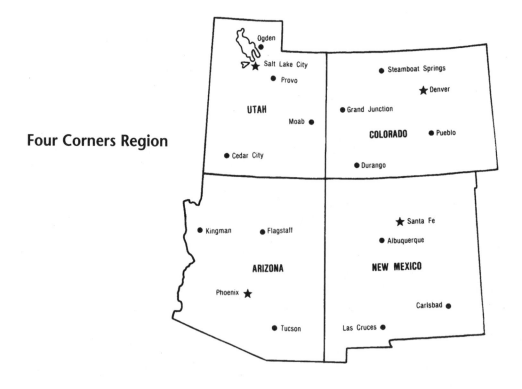

Four Corners Region

■ Study the maps and answer the questions below.

1. The Four Corners Region is mostly a region of _____ and

_____ .

2. Who owns most of the land in Utah?_____

3. List three important National Parks in the Four Corners region.

_____

_____

_____

4. Why do you think this region is not densely populated?

_____

5. Name one Indian tribe that lives in this region. _____

6. Why is water a scarce resource in this region? _____

7. What is Denver's major source of water?_____

8. Could a scarce water supply keep the region's population from growing in the future?

_____

9. On the map on page 76, circle the names of the four capital cities.

10. On the map below, darken the four states of the Four Corners region.

The United States

Pacific Southwest Region

Two states make up the Pacific Southwest region. These states are California and Nevada. California is a state of contrasts. It has both the highest and the lowest points in the 48 *contiguous* states (those states that have shared boundaries). The highest point, at 14,494 feet, is Mt. Whitney in the Sierra Nevadas. The lowest point, at 282 feet below sea level, is in Death Valley.

California's population of almost 30 million people is larger than the entire population of Canada. There are several major population centers: Los Angeles, San Francisco, and San Diego. There are many smaller cities, too.

People have come from all over the United States and the world to live in California. Some came there looking for jobs. Others came because of the pleasant climate.

Nevada, too, is a vacationland for many Americans. The state is also famous for its gold mines. These mines produce about 66% of all the gold mined in the United States each year.

■ Answer the questions below.

1. What is the population of California?

   _____

2. List two reasons why people came to live in California.

   _____

   _____

   _____

   _____

3. List two things that Nevada is famous for.

   _____

   _____

4. How much gold is mined each year in Nevada?

   _____

Pacific Southwest Region

5. What does the term *contiguous* mean? _____

_____

6. List two large cities in California.

_____

7. List two cities in Nevada.

_____

8. What is the lowest point in California? _____

9. California's population is larger than that of what foreign country? _____

10. What "four corners" states border on California and Nevada? _____

_____

11. What body of water borders California to the west? You may need an atlas to help you.

_____

12. Label the Sierra Nevadas on the map on page 78.
    Use the map on page 29 to help you.

13. What is the highest point in California? How high is it?_____

14. On the map on page 78, circle the names of the two capital cities.

15. Darken the states of the Pacific Southwest region on the map below.

The United States

U
N
I
T

5

There are five states in the Pacific Northwest region. These states are Washington, Oregon, Idaho, Montana, and Wyoming. This region was explored by Lewis and Clark in the early 1800s. Later, thousands of settlers traveled the Oregon Trail to build homes in the Pacific Northwest.

Many famous national parks are located in the Pacific Northwest. Yellowstone National Park in Wyoming is famous for its beautiful mountain scenery and *geysers,* or springs that spout hot water and steam into the air. Old Faithful Geyser, the best known of Yellowstone's geysers, attracts millions of visitors each year.

The Pacific Northwest region also is known for its huge forests. Oregon and Washington together produce almost one fourth of the lumber in the United States. The U.S. Forest Service manages thousands of acres of timberland in these states.

Timber is not the only natural resource in this region. The Rocky Mountains contain vast mineral deposits. Lead, gold, silver, and copper as well as oil and natural gas are found in large quantities there.

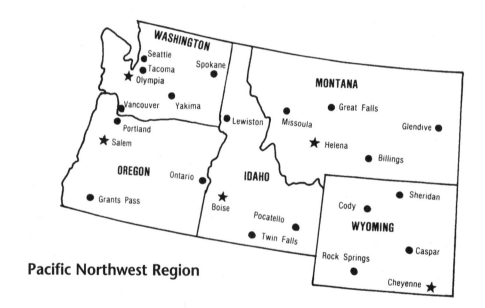

Pacific Northwest Region

Answer the questions below.

1. Who explored this region in the early 1800s? _____

2. What famous trail took settlers to the Pacific Northwest region? _____

3. What is one attraction in Yellowstone National Park? _____

_____

4. How much of the nation's lumber is produced in Washington and Oregon?

_____

5. List three valuable mineral resources that are mined in this region.

_____

6. List two jobs that people in this region might have. _____

_____

7. What does the U.S. Forest Service do in this region? _____

_____

8. List the Pacific Northwest states that border on Canada. _____

_____

9. Parts of this region have extremely low population density.
   What have you just read that might explain why?

_____

_____

10. List the two Pacific Northwest states that border the Pacific Ocean.

_____

11. On the map on page 80, circle the names of the five capital cities.

12. Darken the states of the Pacific Northwest region on the map below.

The United States

Alaska is the largest state in the United States. It is also the northernmost state. Much of Alaska lies north of the Arctic Circle. Its far north location makes the daylight hours very short in the winter and very long in the summer. In some locations in northern Alaska, the sun never completely sets for a few days during the summer!

Alaska is a land of contrasts. Most of the state is still wilderness. In those areas, the *population density* is very low. Yet part of Alaska along the *panhandle* (it is called the "panhandle" because it looks like a handle on a pan) has small growing cities. This part of Alaska has a high *population density*. These cities look like other American cities in the "lower 48" states. They have traffic jams, expanding businesses, and even tall office buildings.

Alaska is famous for its oil deposits. These oil deposits are located along the north slope. The north slope is the Arctic coastline of the state. To get the oil to refineries, oil companies have built a pipeline. The pipeline, which is more than 800 miles long, runs from Prudhoe Bay on the Arctic coast to Valdez on the Pacific Ocean. Alaskans earn a lot of money from these oil deposits. The oil industry has brought many jobs to the people of Alaska.

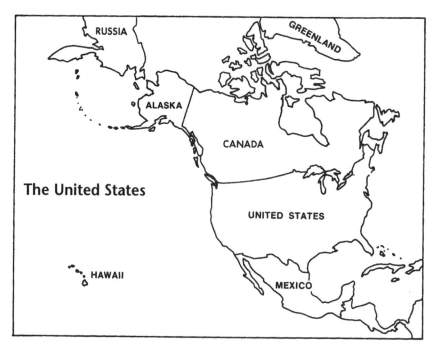

Study both maps and answer the questions.

1. Shade in Alaska on the above map.

2. Label the Arctic Ocean, the Atlantic Ocean, and the Pacific Ocean.

3. On the map below, circle the part of Alaska called the "panhandle."

4. List the names of two rivers in Alaska. _____

_____

5. During what season of the year are the Alaskan days very long?

_____

_____

6. What mineral is Alaska famous for today? _____

7. What two places does the Alaskan pipeline connect? Circle them on your map.

a. _____   b. _____

8. Why did the oil companies need to build a pipeline?

_____

_____

9. List one way in which oil deposits are important to the people of Alaska.

_____

10. Why do you think very few people live in Alaska?

_____

_____

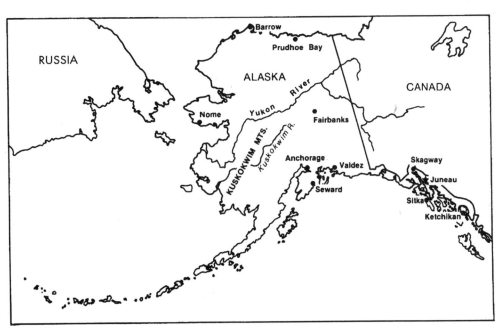

Region of Alaska

Region of Hawaii

The state of Hawaii is different from the other 49 states. It is the only state that is made up entirely of islands. These islands are located in the Pacific Ocean. More than 130 islands of many sizes make up the state of Hawaii. The islands stretch more than 1,600 miles from east to west.

The Hawaiian Islands were formed by volcanic activity. These volcanic forces are still at work on the Big Island, the island of Hawaii. There, Mauna Loa sends hot lava streaming down the sides of the volcano. Tourists come from the other 49 states to the Hawaii Volcanoes National Park to see this active volcano. Tourism is an important industry in Hawaii today.

Many different kinds of crops grow in Hawaii. The islands are famous for their sugar cane and pineapple plantations. Papayas, macadamia nuts, coffee, and flowers, especially orchids, also provide income for Hawaiians.

The people of Hawaii have come from many parts of the world. In the nineteenth century, people from China, Japan, Portugal, Korea, and the Philippine Islands came to work on the sugar cane and pineapple plantations. In the twentieth century, American families in the military came to Hawaii. One of America's most famous navy bases is located at Pearl Harbor on the island of Oahu.

 Study the map below and answer the questions.

1. Circle the Hawaiian Islands on the above map.

2. How many islands are there in the state of Hawaii? _____

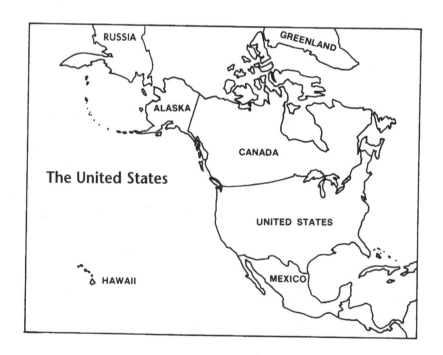

3. What makes Hawaii different from the other 49 states? _____

_____

4. How many miles from east to west is the state of Hawaii? _____

5. What natural force formed the Hawaiian Islands? _____

_____

6. On what island can you see an active volcano? _____

7. List two crops that are important in the state of Hawaii.

    a. _____

    b. _____

8. What famous naval base is located on the island of Oahu?

_____

9. List two reasons why people have come up to live in Hawaii.

    a. _____

    b. _____

10. In what ways do tourists bring more income to Hawaiians? _____

_____

_____

The Major Hawaiian Islands

Economic Regions—U.S. Agricultural Regions

In addition to grouping the United States into regions by states, geographers sometimes look at the United States in terms of its economic life. Agriculture is one important part of the U.S. economy. Geographers are interested in the different agricultural regions in the U.S.

Wheat-Growing Regions in the United States

A Answer the questions.

1. What does this map show? _____

_____

2. Which two states use the most land for growing wheat?

   a. _____

   b. _____

3. Name five other states in which wheat is a major crop.

   a. _____

   b. _____

   c. _____

   d. _____

   e. _____

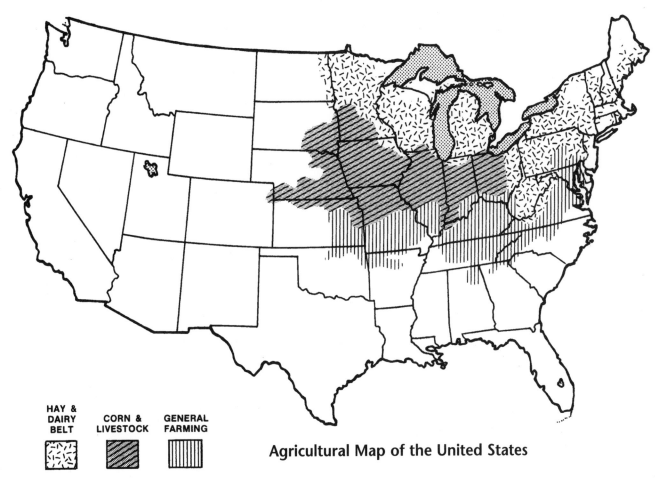

HAY &
DAIRY
BELT

CORN &
LIVESTOCK

GENERAL
FARMING

Agricultural Map of the United States

B Study the map and answer the questions.

1. List eight states in which dairy farming is a major agricultural activity. _____

_____

2. Why do you think hay is raised in a dairy-farming region? _____

_____

3. List five states in which general farming is most common. _____

_____

4. List five states in the *Corn Belt.*_____

_____

Ethnic Neighborhoods in Cities

Geographers are also interested in where people of different nationalities and *ethnic* backgrounds live. People from all over the world have come to live in the United States. Many of these people first make their homes in the big cities. Often they will live in a neighborhood where other people from their country are already living. Geographers try to discover where these different *ethnic neighborhoods* are found.

Many of the ethnic neighborhoods of our cities are famous. Almost every large city, for example, has an area called *Chinatown.* Visitors to the city like to come to Chinatown to enjoy the restaurants and the special holiday celebrations.

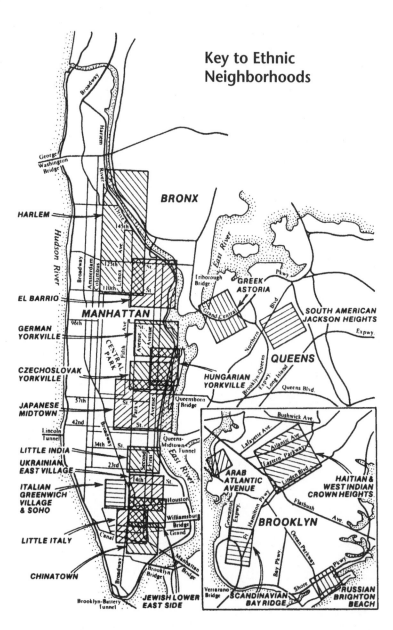

Key to Ethnic Neighborhoods

New York City is home to more different kinds of people than any other city in the world. These people brought their different foods and customs with them to New York. A visitor to New York can have breakfast in Japan, lunch in Italy, and dinner in India without ever leaving the city!

In the earlier years of immigration, such ethnic neighborhoods were clearly distinct. Today, they are less defined in some cities and more evident in others. Through ethnic neighborhoods, people can preserve their special culture, foods, and language. Visiting an ethnic neighborhood lets others share in a heritage that may vary from their own.

Study the map on page 88 and answer the questions.

1. What does the phrase *ethnic neighborhood* mean? _____

_____

2. What does the term *Chinatown* mean? _____

_____

3. How can you eat in many different countries without ever leaving New York City?

_____

_____

4. How might an ethnic neighborhood help preserve a culture's customs? _____

_____

_____

5. List six examples of ethnic neighborhoods found in New York City.

a. _____

b. _____

c. _____

d. _____

e. _____

f. _____

6. What might you learn if you visited an ethnic neighborhood in one of America's cities?

_____

_____

7. What groups do you think probably live in these ethnic neighborhoods?

a. German Yorktown _____

b. Little Italy _____

c. Spanish Harlem _____

d. Greek Astoria _____

e. Little India _____

Congressional Districts

UNIT 5

The number of representatives a state has in the United States House of Representatives is based on the population of the state.

When a state has more than one representative, congressional districts have to be set up. The voters in one part of the state choose one representative to represent them in the House. In another part of the state, the voters there choose another representative to represent them. Boundary lines of congressional districts have to be drawn so that the voters know which representative is theirs.

These congressional districts are *political regions.* As the population increases or decreases in a state, the boundary lines of the congressional districts change. Some districts cover very large areas. Other districts are very small in size. However, the number of people in each district, by law, must be about the same.

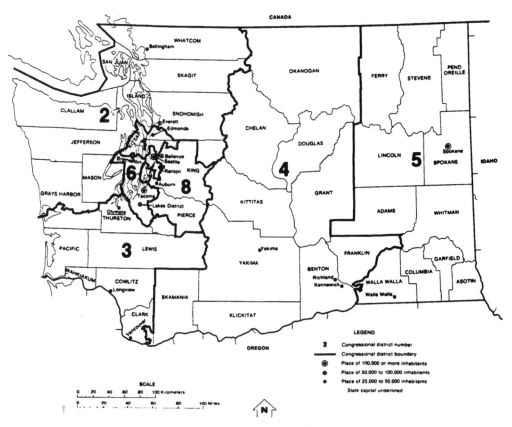

Congressional Districts in Washington State

Study the map on page 90. Answer the following questions.

1. What is the name of the map on page 90? _____

2. How many congressional districts does Washington state have? _____

3. Are these districts equal in area? _____

4. Which district covers the largest area? _____

5. Which district covers the smallest area? _____

6. Look carefully at the map. Which district do the people of Seattle live in?

   _____

7. Which district do the people of Spokane live in?

   _____

8. There are not many towns in District 4. Give one reason why there are not many towns there.

   _____

   _____

9. In what district is the population density high?

   _____

   _____

10. In what district do you think there might be many farms? Why?

   _____

   _____

11. What country borders Washington state on the north?

   _____

12. How many representatives does each district have? _____

Careers in Geography

Geographers have many different kinds of jobs in the United States today. Most people think that geographers spend their time making maps. Some geographers are mapmakers. They are called *cartographers*. The National Geographic Society, for example, hires cartographers to make the maps in its magazine. Many government agencies hire cartographers. The Defense Department needs maps for the United States military forces to use. The Department of Transportation needs maps of the nation's highways and airways. The Department of Agriculture needs maps that show different temperature, soil, and rainfall in the regions to help the nation's farmers.

Not all geographers, however, are cartographers. Many geographers work for private industry. They help businesses decide where the best place to build a new factory would be. They do studies of where customers live. They tell retail stores how far customers might be willing to travel to get to their stores.

Other geographers work to prevent pollution. They study wind patterns to see whether an area is being harmed by air pollutants. They study water systems to track down the sources of water pollution. They work for state and local governments to try to improve the quality of the environment.

Geography is a very interesting field. Geographers find out about almost every area of human activity.

■ Answer the questions below.

1. What does a cartographer do? _____

2. List two places where a cartographer might work.

_____

_____

3. Why might an industry hire a geographer? _____

4. Why might a retail store hire a geographer? _____

5. How does a geographer work to improve the environment? _____

_____

6. List three different types of maps that a cartographer might design. _____

_____

7. Why does the Department of Defense need maps? _____

_____

End-of-Book Test

A Write the letter of the term next to its definition.

a. lines of latitude
b. contiguous
c. weather
d. prime meridian
e. region
f. population density

g. cartographer
h. tributary
i. geography
j. acid rain
k. compass
l. river system

m. equator
n. climate
o. lines of longitude
p. megalopolis
q. immigrant
r. map

_____ 1. the number of people who live on each square mile of land

_____ 2. a main river and all the other rivers that flow into it

_____ 3. a person who moves to a new country from another country

_____ 4. a representation of a real place on the earth's surface

_____ 5. giant city

_____ 6. average or normal weather conditions of a place over a long time

_____ 7. a drawing on a map that shows which direction is north

_____ 8. pollution from smoke mixed with precipitation

_____ 9. imaginary lines that go across the earth's surface

_____ 10. zero degree line of latitude

_____ 11. sharing boundaries

_____ 12. the study of the earth and its resources and the way in which people use those resources

_____ 13. an area with a lot of features that are alike or similar

_____ 14. daily changes in temperature, wind, cloudiness, and precipitation in a particular place

_____ 15. zero degree line of longitude

_____ 16. imaginary lines that go up and down on the earth's surface

_____ 17. a mapmaker

_____ 18. a smaller river that flows into a main river

B Underline the term that completes each sentence.

1. Political geographers might study people's (voting patterns, religions).

2. To become skilled at geography, you must learn how to read and use (maps, newspapers).

3. The temperature zone of the Arctic is the (mid-latitude regions, polar regions).

4. Congressional districts are determined by (population, area).

5. A state that has five people per square mile has (low, high) population density.

6. Georgia is located in the (New England, Southeast) region.

7. If you are facing south, the direction to your right is (west, east).

8. Hawaii is made up entirely of (islands, deserts).

9. Because of the (telephone, telegraph), the pony express mail service did not last very long.

10. An area that gets very little rainfall is called a (plain, desert).

C Answer the following questions about the map below.

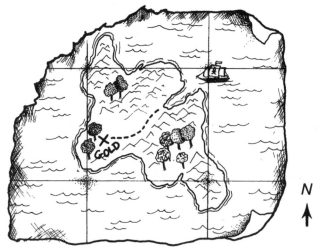

1. What is shown on the map? _____

2. Once you left your ship and landed on the coast, which direction would

   you walk to get to the X?_____

3. If you faced west at the X, what would you see?_____

4. Which direction would you walk from the X if you wanted to get to the largest forest?

   _____

5. What is southeast of the largest forest? _____

6. From the largest forest, which direction would you walk to return to your ship? _____

D Write either *True* or *False* next to each statement.

_____ 1. The St. Lawrence Seaway connects the Atlantic Ocean
                       and the Great Lakes.

_____ 2. An economic geographer is interested in areas where people earn
                       their living in similar ways.

_____ 3. The physical characteristics of the United States tell what the people
                       of the United States are like.

_____ 4. The northernmost state in the United States is Alaska.

_____ 5. The term *Rust Belt* refers to areas where old forests are dying out.

_____ 6. Today most cargo is loaded onto ships by longshoremen.

_____ 7. The drawing on a map that shows which direction is north
                       is called a *cardinal.*

_____ 8. It is faster to fly than to drive from Chicago to New York.

_____ 9. Illinois is located in the Great Lakes region.

_____ 10. The zero degree line of latitude is called the *prime meridian.*

E Use the map below to answer the following questions.

1. What is the temperature in Raleigh? _____

2. Is it snowing in Billings? _____

3. What city has the warmest temperature? _____

4. Is it warmer in Boise or Boston? _____

5. Is it raining in Houston? _____

F Look at the map of the 48 contiguous states. Then answer the questions.

1. What are the five lakes in the north central region called as a group?

_____

2. What are the names of the three states on the Pacific coast?

_____

3. What ocean lies to the east of the United States?

_____

4. What is the northernmost state on the East Coast?

_____

5. What country lies to the north of the United States? to the south?

_____

6. What is the largest state on the map?

_____

G Answer these questions.

1. How does a grid system help geographers find places? _____

_____

2. What kinds of information can maps be used to show? _____

_____